A Timeline Bo

A GUIDED TOUR THROUGH HISTORY

New Orleans

RANDI MINETOR

Photographs by Nic Minetor

travel

Guilford, Connecticut

An imprint of Globe Pequot Press

Original base maps provided by Compass Maps, Ltd.
Updated maps and tour maps by Nick Trotter © Morris Book Publishing, LLC.
Historical PopOut map courtesy of the Library of Congress.
All photographs © Nic Minetor except for the following: Photos on pp. 4, 8, 10, 17 (top), 21, 38, 40, 42 (top and bottom), 43, 44, 45, 46, 61, 62, 63, 64, 75, and 76 courtesy of the Library of Congress; photos on pp. 9 (top), 11, 18 (top and bottom), 19, 20 (top and bottom), and 37 (top and bottom) courtesy of the Louisiana State Museum; photo on p. 9 (bottom) courtesy of the National World War II Museum, New Orleans; and photos on pp. 12, 85, 86, and 89 from Wikimedia Commons.

Library of Congress Cataloging-in-Publication Data is available on file.

ISBN 978-0-7627-5739-8

Printed in China
10 9 8 7 6 5 4 3 2 1

All the information in this guidebook is subject to change. We recommend that you call ahead to obtain current information before traveling. All restaurants are open daily for breakfast, lunch, and dinner, unless otherwise noted.

Contents

Entwined grillwork is one of
the hallmarks of the Vieux
Carré's old world architecture.

Introduction

Say the name "New Orleans," and a collage of images come immediately to mind, as vivid as the purple, green, and gold of its most famous annual celebration: the wild spectacle of Mardi Gras, its beads, feathers, floats, and music as full of life as any city could ever hope to be. Think of New Orleans, and hear the music that sprang from a park in which slaves and free people of color amassed every Sunday, beating the syncopated rhythms of their distant homelands and sending up a jubilant sound that drew spectators and listeners from all corners of the Mississippi floodplain.

Think of the Crescent City and feel your mouth begin to water in anticipation of the extraordinary flavors to come, blended by the merging of Louisianan cultures: the pungent aromas of cayenne and cumin, the heat of andouille and boudin sausage, the sweet crunchiness of pralines, the tender meat of crawfish and gulf shrimp. Picture New Orleans and envision skillfully entwined grillwork forming balcony railings on square-faced houses, each home abutting the next in a style we associate with the old cities in Spain or France—two countries that bore heavy influence on traditional New Orleans architecture and lifestyle.

The city's deep roots in both French and Spanish cultures form only a fraction of its foundation, however: New Orleans draws on eighteenth-century Caribbean and African mores and customs, as well as those of the Native Americans who preceded the white man by millennia on this land. The result is a pastiche that's entirely new, going beyond the American

French and Spanish influences give New Orleans architecture its distinction.

Opposite: Nothing says New Orleans like the Mardi Gras jester.

Your bananas Foster is prepared tableside at Brennan's, one of the city's finest restaurants.

melting pot to forge two entirely unique cultures in Louisiana's ethnic foundry.

A visit to New Orleans takes on both the reverence of a pilgrimage and the exotic wonder of an adventure, combining the opportunity to explore some of the nation's earliest history with the complete abandon demanded by the city's slogan, "*Laissez les bon temps roulez!*" The good times roll day and night in this sleepless town, from the noisily uninhibited crowds on Bourbon Street to the river that's ever in motion—the mighty Mississippi that served as the central artery for a fledgling country.

NEW ORLEANS	1500	1600		1700		
	1541 Hernando De Soto "discovers" the Mississippi River for Spain.	**1682** Robert de La Salle claims the area for the French.	**1699** First Mardi Gras celebrated.	**1718** First settlement established in New Orleans.	**1720** First slaves arrive; first levees constructed.	**1721** French Quarter designed by Adrien de Pauger; first deported French convicts arrive.

New Orleans' founders knew the city would become a major port.

The City at the End of the River

Perched precariously on the banks of the Mississippi River just one hundred miles from its mouth, New Orleans was founded with some understanding of its potential fate: Even the earliest European settlers recognized that a city at sea level or below would forever be in danger of destruction. Yet in such a strategic location, a short distance upstream from the junction of the continent's major shipping lane and the Gulf of Mexico, a city would prosper in spite of the potential for disaster—and to the French who claimed ownership of the river and many miles of adjoining land to either side of it, there was no option but to build.

1765	1766	1769	1776	1788	1790	1791	1796
First Acadians arrive from Nova Scotia.	New Orleans colonists revolt against Spanish rule.	Spain quashes uprising, takes control of New Orleans.	American Revolution begins.	Fire destroys French architecture throughout city.	New Orleans opens trade with U.S.	Caribbean refugees from Saint Domingue (Haiti) begin to arrive.	Birth of granulated sugar industry.

The first New Orleans settlement took advantage of its waterside location.

The Native Americans who preceded the French on this saturated land knew full well the opportunities such a location presented. Small clans of hunters gravitated here to the edge of the river, forming large farming communities and bartering food and goods between them. The river and its easy access to the Gulf of Mexico afforded these communities a great deal of freedom to travel for trade, widening their territory by land and water and facilitating the exchange of cultural mores, religious rites, and customs of daily life as well as goods. Among the remains of these clans are artifacts that came from the faraway lands of Central and South America.

When the French arrived here in the late 1600s, they had already secured the St. Lawrence River and Great Lakes well to the north, with the understanding that control of the waterways in this untamed New World would

1800							
1800 Spain cedes Louisiana to France.	**1803** France sells Louisiana Purchase to U.S.	**1805** James Pitot improves Carondelet Canal; New Orleans becomes an important port.	**1812** Louisiana becomes a U.S. state.	**1815** Battle of New Orleans is last in War of 1812.	**1830s** More than 1,000 steamboats per year dock in New Orleans.	**1833** First official Mardi Gras celebration.	**1857** Mistick Krewe of Comus holds first parade.

mean control over the entire region's commerce. France had claimed the northern lands along the Mississippi River in 1672; ten years later, explorer Robert de LaSalle and eighteen Native Americans left Illinois in canoes and headed down the river to its mouth. La Salle claimed the entire area for France and naming it La Louisiane to honor the current king of France, Louis XIV. Subsequent expeditions did not fare as well: When La Salle attempted to return to the Mississippi River from France in 1684 with four ships and three hundred colonists, his plans were foiled by pirates, navigation issues, and natives determined to keep him from making landfall. In the end, La Salle and his colonists settled on what is now the Texas coast, and La Salle died at the hands of a mutineer in 1687 without ever relocating the river.

To make the most of the country's holdings in the New World, the next logical move for France was colonization—creating settlements from which they could explore their land, determine what resources it contained, and establish a permanent presence on the largely uncharted continent.

First on France's agenda was residency at the mouth of the Mississippi River. The men chosen by France to sail to the southern port already lived in New France: Pierre Le Moyne d'Iberville and his brother, Jean-Baptiste Le Moyne de Bienville. Working their way along the northern Gulf of Mexico coastline and exploring the largest islands along the way—islands that are now part of Gulf Islands National Seashore—d'Iberville and Bienville established a colony at Fort Maurepas (now Ocean Springs, Mississippi) in 1699. Bienville would remain in La Louisiane to found another colony at Mobile, Alabama, and to continue his exploration of the river's mouth. It would be 1717 before he would have the opportunity to discover the crescent in the river where he would found New Orleans.

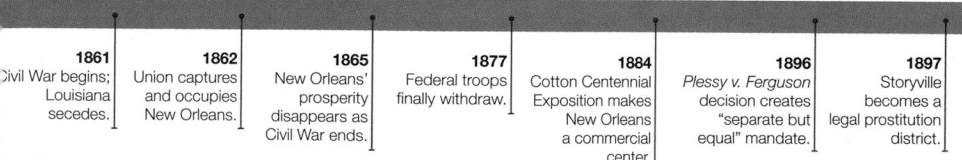

1861	**1862**	**1865**	**1877**	**1884**	**1896**	**1897**
Civil War begins; Louisiana secedes.	Union captures and occupies New Orleans.	New Orleans' prosperity disappears as Civil War ends.	Federal troops finally withdraw.	Cotton Centennial Exposition makes New Orleans a commercial center.	Plessy v. Ferguson decision creates "separate but equal" mandate.	Storyville becomes a legal prostitution district.

Today St. Louis Cathedral represents the faith and determination of the first permanent settlers.

The Impossible City

What makes the Mississippi Delta such a difficult place to put a major city? Most international capitals came to be because of a significant waterway adjacent to the site, and New Orleans certainly fits this description. However, in most cases, these cities grew up on the edge of a bay, or at a narrowing of a river at which a bridge or other means of crossing can be constructed. The Mississippi River Delta, however, provides neither of these: The river does not narrow from its mouth all the way to central Illinois, and the delta becomes a labyrinth of channels that are just as likely to lead to mud and

1900

1917
Storyville is closed at request of U.S. Navy.

1933
Five New Orleans banks fail in Great Depression.

1941
World War II makes New Orleans a ship-building hub.

1945
J&M Recording Studio launches.

1958
Pontchartrain Expressway leads to suburban development.

1965
Voting Rights Act opens political office to people of color.

1967
New Orleans Saints join the National Football League.

swampland as they are to connect with the river. Worse, this mushy muck-land extends far out into the Gulf of Mexico, creating treacherous passage for large ships.

Bienville's discovery of the bend in the river provided a partial solution, a place to construct a small port city on the natural levee the Mississippi creates. Today, when we visit the French Quarter, we can wander through the city Bienville imagined and settlers built, a sixty-six-block town just a few feet above sea level, with plenty of waterfront to turn into a significant port.

Since the city's founding in 1718, inventors have created technologies that keep the lower lands free of swamp water and used modern engineer-ing techniques to contain the river and keep it from creating new courses for itself—something the Mississippi did for many millennia before human concentrations forced its containment. Major storms and flooding came to New Orleans even before the catastrophic events of 2005, and the city found its footing again and again atop its mucky foundation. Today, we can see the city rising once more, its cultural and entertainment districts back at full force and its residential neighborhoods working their way back from the bursting of the levees during Hurricane Katrina's storm surge.

New Orleans may be battered and bruised, but its spangles still sparkle and the experience it affords tourists is still one of the most lively and excit-ing in the country. Whether you come to New Orleans to explore its history, its one-of-a-kind cuisine, its legendary music, its links to voodoo's myster-ies, or its spectacular Mardi Gras celebrations, you will find a city deter-mined to retain all of the qualities that led to its most recent nickname: the Big Easy.

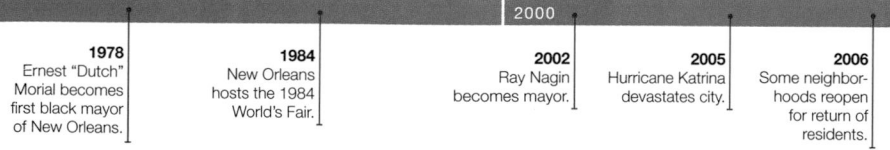

2000				
1978	**1984**	**2002**	**2005**	**2006**
Ernest "Dutch" Morial becomes first black mayor of New Orleans.	New Orleans hosts the 1984 World's Fair.	Ray Nagin becomes mayor.	Hurricane Katrina devastates city.	Some neighbor-hoods reopen for return of residents.

Key Participants in New Orleans History

Louis Armstrong The greatest of the jazz greats from New Orleans, Armstrong's influence in the earliest days of jazz makes him one of the inventors of a uniquely American and heavily New Orleans–influenced musical style. His skill on the cornet and trumpet, combined with his winning personality and his astonishing musical spontaneity, made him a professional musician by the age of sixteen, playing in the bars of Storyville and coming to the attention of the era's band leaders. As Armstrong's career ramped up with the advent of recorded music, he moved to New York City to play in Fletcher Henderson's Orchestra and became a sought-after session man for dozens of records. By 1925 he began recording under his own name, and Louis Armstrong and His Orchestra became one of the most desirable acts of the swing era. Armstrong's own success continued through the 1940s and 1950s—and when he recorded his own version of the title song from the Broadway hit *Hello, Dolly,* he shoved the Beatles out of the number-one slot in the popular Top 40. Another generation would learn to love Armstrong when he recorded "What a Wonderful World" in 1968. He was still hailed as the greatest jazz musician of all time when he died quietly at home in New York in 1971.

New Orleans

Jean-Baptiste Le Moyne, Sieur de Bienville Born in Montreal in 1680, Bienville was a French citizen who founded New Orleans in 1718 while he served as the French-appointed governor of the Louisiana colonies. One of four brothers who played significant roles in the development of the area around the Mississippi River Delta, Bienville sailed to the river's mouth on a ship captained by his brother, Pierre d'Iberville, who would lead colonization in the area that is now Biloxi. Bienville's tumultuous leadership of the earliest colonies—including four separate terms as the territory's governor—landed him in a world of conflict and adventure, during which he discovered the bend in the Mississippi River that became the site of the colony's capital, the city of New Orleans.

John Howard Ferguson *See* Homer Plessy.

Andrew Jackson Higgins The flamboyant entrepreneur who owned Higgins Industries took on the challenge of designing a boat that could ferry soldiers, jeeps, and tanks from ships at sea directly onto the beaches on the coast of France and North Africa, and onto the Pacific atolls in the Philippines and Guam. Thanks to the Higgins boats, the Allies could avoid costly, deadly attacks before landing an assault force, making these boats invaluable in every major American amphibious operation in World War II. Higgins is widely credited with making the invasion of Normandy possible on June 6, 1944, giving the Allies a significant advantage and turning the tide of the war in Europe. General Dwight Eisenhower was heard to call Higgins "the man who won the war for us."

Andrew Jackson Commander of the U.S. forces in 1815 during the Battle of New Orleans, Jackson would go on to lead a military campaign against the Seminole Indians in 1817, a precursor to his involvement in summarily removing American Indians from the southern states as the seventh president of the United States. Nicknamed Old Hickory for his unwavering strength on the battlefield, Jackson acquired his hatred for the British during the Revolutionary War, when he and his brother Robert were captured and nearly starved to death by English regulars. Jackson served as solicitor of the Western District from 1788 to 1791, and became solicitor for the territory of Tennessee the following year—making him the first U.S. president to have a direct connection with America's frontier. He was elected president in 1828, and served until 1837.

Jean Lafitte Partner in the smuggling business with his brother, Pierre, Jean ran a warehouse in New Orleans in 1805 from which he distributed the stolen merchandise his brother acquired. When Congress passed the Embargo Act of 1807, Jean and Pierre went looking for a new port to continue their operations, settling on Barataria, an island off the coast of Louisiana. Eventually, the brothers became pirates and privateers, clearing ships at sea of their goods but treating the captive crews well—even returning their ships to them once the pirates had the merchandise. Jean's reputation swelled, however, and he had several encounters with the law before General Andrew Jackson approached him to request the service of Lafitte and all of his men in the coming Battle of New Orleans, the last battle of the War of 1812.

Lafitte traded clemency for his men in exchange for their service, and when he and his men proved to be a valiant, pivotal fighting force, they all received full pardons.

Marie Laveau Probably the most famous practitioner of voodoo in New Orleans, Laveau was born in 1801, the daughter of a free Creole woman of color and a white farmer. Often confused with her daughter of the same name, Laveau the elder's life history is shrouded in mystery, rumor, and tall tales, but we do know that she skillfully blended practices of Roman Catholicism with African religion to concoct her own seemingly magical rites. Some say she had a snake named for the African god Zombi, while others guess that her magic was actually manipulation made possible through her knowledge of the backstairs of rich people's home lives. Whether she learned their secrets through a network of informants has never been proven conclusively, but chances are good her information came through her work as a hairdresser, a profession that preceded bartending as the keeper of customers' secrets.

Cosimo Matassa Founder of J&M Recording Studio, where greats from Little Richard to Ray Charles got their start, Matassa receives credit as the most influential figure in New Orleans jazz history for his ability to bring musicians' work to a mass audience. In the back of his Sicilian parents' store on the French Quarter's Rampart Street, Matassa shaped a sound that would become synonymous with New Orleans music, emphasizing drums and bass over piano and horn and featuring vocalists that became legends in the industry. Among his many recordings, Matassa laid down Fats Domino's "The Fat Man" and "My Blue Heaven," Little Richard's "Tutti Frutti" and "Long Tall Sally," and dozens of other seminal cuts.

Ernest N. "Dutch" Morial A New Orleans native and a leading advocate for civil rights, Morial became the first black mayor of New Orleans in 1978. Creole by ancestry, Morial was the first African-American to earn a law degree from Louisiana State University, going on to serve as president of the local NAACP chapter in the 1960s. As mayor, he presided over strikes by sanitation workers and police, introduced hiring quotas that opened civil and construction jobs to people of color, increased the number of black police officers, and achieved federal funding for major developments including Canal Place and other areas of the French Quarter. Always a controversial figure, Morial lost momentum in his second term, especially when the 1984 World's Fair in New Orleans declared bankruptcy while it was still in progress. He died in 1989 while running for a third term.

Clarence Ray Nagin The corruption-busting mayor who was in office when Hurricane Katrina hit New Orleans, Nagin rose from a low-income New Orleans upbringing in which his father worked three jobs to provide his children with a college education. He graduated from Tuskegee University and worked in industry in Los Angeles and Dallas before returning to New Orleans in 1985 as controller of Cox New Orleans, a company he would steer back into prosperity. In 2002, he campaigned for mayor on a platform of political reform, vowing to run the city like a business—and he came from behind to win the election and enact the anti-corruption programs he'd promised. Nagin rose to international prominence in the last days of August 2005, when Hurricane Katrina passed through the city and he ordered the first mandatory evacuation in New Orleans' history. His response to the city's devastation and its aftermath has been widely criti-cized by politicians, historians, and the media, but New Orleans residents voted him in for a second term in 2006.

Adrien de Pauger Selected by Bienville in 1721 as the designer of the French Quarter, Pauger was an assistant engineer who followed Le Blond de La Tour as the principal architect of the new city when La Tour and Bienville could not resolve their disagreements. Well respected by his colleagues, Pauger led a group of select engineers and work-men who came to the new colony at the behest of the Indies Company, and supervised construction of a 62-foot wooden pyramid at La Balize before continuing to New Orleans. Pauger's original design for the eleven-by-seven-block French Quarter included many of the street names we see today: Royale, d'Iberville, de Chartres, Bourbon, d'Orleans, and St. Louis.

James Pitot The second mayor of New Orleans, the French-born and educated Pitot fled from France during the French Revolution and settled in Philadelphia, where he became a U.S. citizen. He arrived in New Orleans in 1796, and came up

James Pitot lived in this house in Mid-City.

through the community ranks as a wealthy merchant and city council member before receiving the appointment of mayor in 1804. Pitot used his savvy as a successful businessman to open New Orleans as an important trade center, addressing issues with the 1.6-mile Carondelet Canal that kept this shallow waterway from working effectively as a shipping lane. The improvements Pitot ordered cleared the way for New Orleans to become a major port along the Mississippi River.

Homer Plessy and John Howard Ferguson

America owes the designation of "separate but equal" accommodations for white and black people to a legal dispute between these two New Orleans residents. On June 7, 1892, Homer

Plessy—who was one-eighth black and seven-eighths white, making him an "octoroon" in the parlance of the day—boarded a railroad car designated for white people only. He refused to leave the car when asked, and his deliberate civil disobedience landed him in jail. Plessy became the defendant in *Homer Adolph Plessy v. The State of Louisiana,* a case in which John Howard Ferguson presided as the judge. Plessy argued that the rule that divided people of color from whites violated the Thirteenth and Fourteenth Amendments, but Ferguson disagreed, ruling that the state had a right to regulate railroads within state boundaries. The case went on to the U.S. Supreme Court, where the justices ruled in favor of Ferguson's decision.

Sidney Story In 1897, in an effort to limit rampant prostitution in New Orleans to a single area, Alderman Story championed a legal prostitution district in New Orleans, bounded by Iberville, Basin, St. Louis, and Robertson Streets. Story wrote the legislation for the district's inception—which included all public houses, bars, and other "businesses of vice"—and in his dubious honor, the locals nicknamed the area "Storyville." While historic records indicate that Story would have liked to include regular medical examinations for prostitutes in his legislation (a common practice in similar European districts), public outcry by women claiming an unjust double standard effectively killed this ordinance—a fact that eventually led to Storyville's demise.

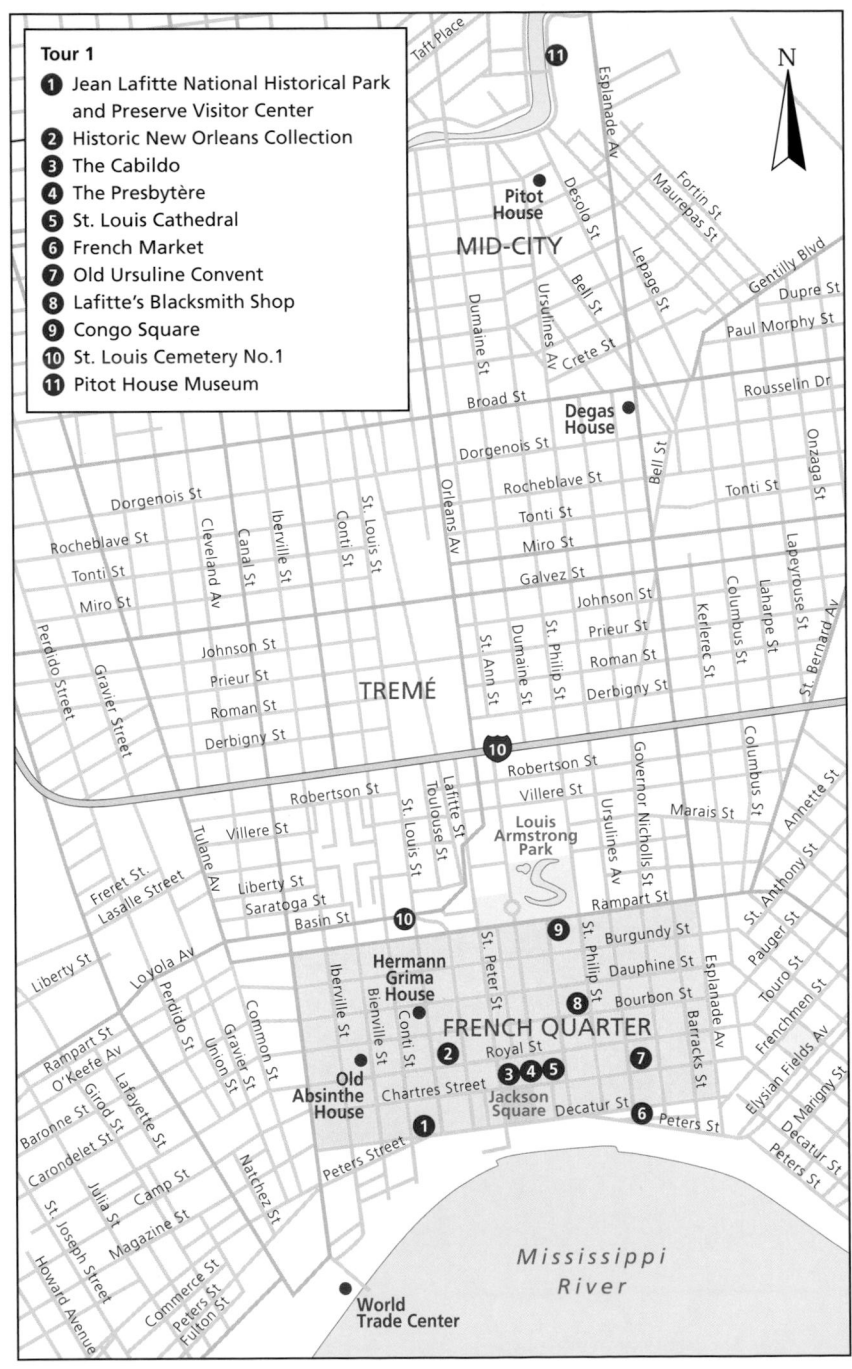

Tour 1
1. Jean Lafitte National Historical Park and Preserve Visitor Center
2. Historic New Orleans Collection
3. The Cabildo
4. The Presbytère
5. St. Louis Cathedral
6. French Market
7. Old Ursuline Convent
8. Lafitte's Blacksmith Shop
9. Congo Square
10. St. Louis Cemetery No.1
11. Pitot House Museum

Tour 1: Pre-1800
A Fetid Swamp Becomes
a Pivotal Port City

Waterways with barely perceptible current, year-round heat and humidity, biting insects, intimidating amphibious creatures sunning themselves on riverbanks . . . this is the territory the expedition originally led by Spanish conquistador Hernando De Soto found when its 400 men arrived here in 1541. The famous explorer may have been the first European to see the mighty Mississippi River, and he was certainly the first to document the discovery. The significance of the event was lost on De Soto, however—the wide, winding river was nothing more than another in a long line of obstacles in the way of his mission. Convinced by hearsay that gold and riches were abundant in the New World, De Soto led a large contingent of Spanish soldiers into undiscovered country to pillage Indian villages, attempt to enslave the natives and persecute them

Hernando De Soto

Bayou St. John is in a neighborhood today, but was surrounded by swampland in 1541.

Robert de La Salle claimed this land for the French.

This stone, discovered in 1910 in Mississippi, may have marked the first French settlement.

until they gave up their hidden wealth. De Soto died in Arkansas in May 1542 without ever finding these nonexistent riches.

More than 140 years would pass before a French explorer would brave the river and travel through the delta region on a more benevolent mission. Robert de La Salle navigated the river on behalf of France in 1682, erecting a cross somewhere around present-day New Orleans. He claimed the land along the Mississippi's western banks for France, naming Louisiana for French King Louis XIV and setting the wheels in motion for the territory's colonization.

With the issues of distance, open seas, fragile sailing ships, and a fairly inhospitable area in which to settle, however, the development of Louisiana happened very gradually, especially by modern standards. Records tell us that a colony on Louisiana's most southern peninsula, Plaquemines Parish, celebrated the New World's first Mardi Gras in 1699, but it would be another nineteen years before a settlement appeared on the southern banks of Lake Pontchartrain.

The man charged with the establishment of the first New Orleans settlement came from a family of explorers, four brothers credited with the leadership of a string of early colonies along the gulf coast. Jean Baptiste Le Moyne, Sieur de Bienville, came to the north-central coast of the Gulf of Mexico on an expedition led by his brother, Pierre Le Moyne d'Iberville. They discovered a number of islands just off the coast before beginning an upstream navigation of the Mississippi River, making it all the way to present-day Baton Rouge before turning back to begin the ocean crossing to France. D'Iberville left two of his brothers in charge of Lousiana: Sauvolle de La Villantry became the territory's first governor, and Bienville served as his second.

The next two decades would prove tumultuous as most of the colonists died of starvation and disease, including Sauvolle. Bienville led the relocation of the colonists to what is now Biloxi, Mississippi, and again to the area that became Mobile, Alabama. In his travels, Bienville discovered a bend in the Mississippi River that looked well protected from hurricanes and tidal waves, and he petitioned the French government for permission to build a settlement there. In 1718, Bienville began construction of La Nouvelle-Orléans, named to honor the Prince Regent of France, Philippe II, Duke of Orléans.

Bienville's brother d'Iberville led the expedition to the Gulf of Mexico.

Planning a City in a Bowl

Seeing the threats to survival of a city flanked on three sides by water, Bienville's first task was to order construction of levees along the Mississippi River. With this forward-thinking operation underway, he could focus on development of a city plan, one that had the potential to turn the higher ground along the water into a thriving commercial center.

Like virtually all efforts to create a settlement in the New World, however, this one was fraught with conflict. Bienville first turned to his chief engineer, Le Blond de la Tour, to design the city, but their disagreements soon led Bienville to decide on an inspired assistant, Adrien de Pauger, to complete the task. De Pauger delivered the fairly simple, rectangular district we now know as the Vieux Carré, or the French Quarter—eleven blocks long

De Pauger's design for New Orleans became the French Quarter.

by seven blocks wide, hugging the banks of the Mississippi River and positioning the new city as a natural stopping place along the continent's major inland waterway. By 1723, France saw fit to move the capital of their holdings in America from Biloxi to New Orleans.

Despite all of Bienville's plans, however, the colony began to fail. The troubles began when King Louis XIV allowed the economic management of Louisiana to go to John Law, a Scotsman and private financier who founded the General Private Bank in France. Law engineered a wild financial scheme that involved, among other things, a gross exaggeration of the value of Louisiana: The original real estate swindler, Law advertised Louisiana as a utopia, deliberately misleading people who bought property on the Gulf of Mexico coast. When people arrived in Louisiana, they found swamps, rampant insects, and oppressive heat, not the paradise they were led to expect.

King Louis XIV

The Code Noir restricted and protected slaves in New Orleans.

Meanwhile, as interest in the colony waned, France began deporting its criminals to New Orleans, beginning in 1721 with eighty-eight prostitutes. Another population found itself in Louisiana, but also not by choice: The first African slaves arrived in 1720, becoming the principal laborers who brought the earliest vestiges of de Pauger's plans into three dimensions.

One of Bienville's most important marks on New Orleans was the adoption of the French government's Code Noir, a set of laws that regulated the rights of slaves in the burgeoning city. Under Code Noir, slave owners had to give their slaves every Sunday off, and the code prevented any physical abuse that went beyond discipline to torture. At the same time, Code Noir took as much as it gave: Slaves could not sell commodities without written permission from their masters, carry anything that might be used as an offensive weapon, or be party to a civil lawsuit. Code Noir also banned any religious practices except for those of the Roman Catholic or Apostolic faiths, calling for the expulsion of Jews from the French colonies.

The French government recalled Bienville in 1725, and he remained in France until 1733. In the meantime, as Law's Company of the Indies dissolved under the weight of its management practices, France imposed restrictions on trade with England, Spain, Mexico, Florida, and the West Indies, dramatically reducing the colony's chances for success. Despite this, commerce thrived after Bienville returned to the colony—mostly because he ignored these trade restrictions altogether. River traffic swelled, making New Orleans an important port between the Mississippi and the Gulf of Mexico.

How the French Colony Became Spanish

The Seven Years War began in 1755, pulling England, France, Spain, and other European countries into a protracted conflict. In the end, French King Louis XV signed the Treaty of Paris on February 10, 1763, ending French colonization and growth in North America and ceding all of Louisiana to Spain—except for New Orleans, which Louis had secretly signed over to his cousin, King Charles III of Spain, the year before as part of the Treaty of Fontainebleau.

This exchange of properties did not sit well with the French residents of Louisiana. In 1766, when Charles sent Spanish governor Don Antonio de Ulloa to Louisiana to assume power, the French settlers drove him out, forcing him to retreat to Cuba. Their success was short-lived, however: Irish-born Spanish general Alexander O'Reilly arrived with two thousand soldiers and twenty-four warships, and captured six leaders of the rebellion, putting them to death on October 25, 1769, at the site of what is now the Old U.S. Mint.

Nova Scotia's Great Upheaval

While the French colonies took shape in the New World's southern regions, a parallel French development far to the north would become a wellspring of cultural influences as its people took to the seas to find a new home.

Over the course of more than a hundred years, sovereignty of the colony known as Acadia bounced from one nationality to another as France, the Netherlands, and Britain battled for the rights to the lands along the Atlantic Ocean. When the French and Indian War began in 1755, the British feared that the French Acadians would take sides against England in the conflict and insisted that every citizen swear an oath of allegiance to the British crown. Just as they feared, the British found themselves with more than six thousand Acadians who refused to swear.

There was nothing to do for it but to dispel the offending residents—so over the next three years, thousands of Acadians were forced to leave their homes in today's Nova Scotia for parts of Canada still owned by the French, or for settlements and cities held by the British well to the south. Some fled to areas that are now Quebec, while others returned to France. Still more found themselves crowded onto ships with destinations all over the eastern coast, scattering family members throughout the continent.

In 1764, when terms of the Treaty of Paris permitted unrestrained emigration from Canada, many more Acadians found their way to Louisiana, which they believed was still a French holding. When they arrived they discovered that France had ceded the region to Spain—but the new governor, Bernardo

Since the 1788 fire, only a few examples remain of French architecture in the French Quarter.

de Galvez, permitted the French-inspired culture to continue without government interference, making the area more than hospitable for the exiled Acadians—and the precise French pronunciation of their original name received an English slurring, renaming them "Cajun."

When a massive fire in 1788 destroyed more than 850 buildings throughout the city of New Orleans, much of the French architecture that remained after the Spanish takeover went up in flames. The construction that replaced the burned buildings maintained a Mediterranean style, but the new structures were built of brick instead of wood, making them more likely to withstand another blaze.

New American Neighbors

By 1790, the United States had become a nation, and New Orleans governor Baron Carondelet granted free trade on the Mississippi to the Americans. New Orleans thrived with this new surge in commerce, making it possible to improve the city with the addition of gas lamps along the streets, drainage ditches to carry waste away from the city, and a police force. A second boon arrived with the invention of mass production of granulated sugar, turning Louisiana's sugar cane production into a flourishing industry.

Word came to New Orleans about a slave uprising in Saint-Domingue, the Caribbean island that we know as Haiti—and in a short time, Caribbean refugees fleeing the island poured into New Orleans, beginning the infusion of island culture into the Louisiana society. With the refugees came a range of new religious practices called *voudou*, a blending of the many polytheistic religions of West African people who came to Saint-Domingue as slaves in the 1500s. The Haitian population became an important element in the merging of African, French, Spanish, and Native American elements in native-born Louisianans, a culture we know as Creole.

On the Way to Statehood

On October 1, 1800, under pressure from First Consul Napoleon Bonaparte of France, Spain ceded the Louisiana Territory to France as part of the secretly negotiated Third Treaty of San Ildefonso. This proved particularly advantageous for Napoleon, who had the territory's entire 828,800 square miles to sell to the United States when he needed funds for his planned conquest of Europe.

The transaction between the soon-to-be emperor and the administration of U.S. President Thomas Jefferson took place on April 30, 1803, with the actual transfer of power completed at the Cabildo, a building that still stands in downtown New Orleans, on December 20 of the same year. Louisiana and a wide swath of North America now belonged to the United States, more than doubling the fledgling country's area with the stroke of a pen.

With the Caribbean refugees came a polytheistic religion called *voudou.*

A Guided Tour through History

Begin your tour at the National Park Service visitor center in the city's French Quarter.

1. Jean Lafitte National Historical Park and Preserve, Laura C. Hudson Visitor Center. The exhibits on the history and conflict that shaped New Orleans provide insights about the city's tumultuous origins, from founding to present day. The emphasis here is on the Acadian and Creole cultures that give the city its character. 419 Decatur Street, (504) 589-3882, www.nps.gov/jela. Daily 9–5. Free. FRENCH QUARTER

2. The Historic New Orleans Collection. There's no better place to gain a comprehensive understanding of the many cultures that originated in New Orleans during its first century than this compact yet comprehensive museum. Take the guided tour of the eleven Louisiana History Galleries, which begin the story in the early eighteenth century, or of the Kemper and Leila Williams House, a combined row house and 1830s cottage transformed in the 1930s when General Williams and his wife decided to invest in the French Quarter to save it from destruction. 533 Royal Street, (504) 523-4662, www.hnoc .org. Museum Tues–Sat 9:30–4:30, Sun 10:30-4:30. Tours Tues–Sat at 10, 11, 2, and 3. Closed national holidays, Good Friday, and Mardi Gras. Museum free; tours $5. FRENCH QUARTER

Tour the Williams House when you visit the Historic New Orleans Collection.

3. The Cabildo. Here in a second-floor room called the Sala Capitular, the governments of France and the United States transferred ownership and power over the Louisiana Territory in 1803, completing the Louisiana Purchase and doubling the size of the United States. The Cabildo's place in history began well before that transaction, however; it served as the capital building of the Spanish Colonial government in New Orleans in the 1700s, and later it became the seat of controversy as the site of the Louisiana State Supreme Court's landmark "separate but equal" ruling in the 1892 *Homer Adolph Plessy v. The State of Louisiana* case. Today it's part of the Louisiana State Museum. Admission includes access to the adjoining Arsenal; you can also purchase a combination ticket to see the Cabildo, the Presbytère, and the Old U.S. Mint for a 20 percent discount. 701 Chartres Street, Jackson Square, (504) 568-6968, http://lsm.crt.state.la.us. Tues–Sun 10–4:30. Adults $6; seniors, students, and active military $5; children 12 and under free. FRENCH QUARTER

In this room, the French and U.S. governments completed the Louisiana Purchase.

The Cabildo houses the Sala Capitular, where many historic events took place, including the Louisiana Purchase.

The Presbytère, now a museum, was constructed as a residence for Capuchin monks.

4. The Presbytère. Originally constructed in 1791 as a home for Capuchin monks, this building is now part of Louisiana State Museum. It showcases a permanent exhibition on the history of Mardi Gras from its earliest origins to the first parades in the nineteenth century, and on to today's spectacular celebration. 751 Chartres Street, Jackson Square, (504) 568-6968, http://lsm.crt.state.la.us. Tues–Sat 9–5. Adults $6; seniors, students, and active military $5; children under 12 free; 20% discount for combination ticket with the Cabildo. FRENCH QUARTER

St. Louis Cathedral is the French Quarter's most recognized landmark.

5. St. Louis Cathedral. Home of the Archdiocese of New Orleans, this is the oldest continuously active Roman Catholic Cathedral in the United

States. The building you see here replaced the original church, which stood here from 1727 until the citywide fire in 1788. Walk in anytime to see the beautifully appointed sanctuary, with its ceiling painted with scenes from the Bible and its stained glass windows that chronicle the life of French King Louis XIV. 615 Pere Antoine Alley, (504) 525-9585, www.stlouiscathedral.org. Open daily during daylight hours for walk-in visitors. Tours Wed–Sat 1–4; call ahead to verify. Free. FRENCH QUARTER

6. The French Market. Since 1791, this area between Decatur Street and the river has been a marketplace to which New Orleans residents came to sell their wares and buy from their neighbors and farmers in the area. Today America's oldest city market flourishes with its boutiques and candy shops, a daily flea market with lots of local souvenirs, strolling musicians, and restaurants. North Peters Street from Esplanade Avenue to Jackson Square, between Decatur Street and the Mississippi River, (504) 522-2621, www.frenchmarket.org. Stores and restaurants keep various hours, but are open daily. FRENCH QUARTER

7. Old Ursuline Convent. The only remaining French Colonial building in the United States, the Ursuline Convent is also the oldest building in the Mississippi River Valley. The Sisters of Ursula arrived in 1727 after a treacherous voyage from France. Once they arrived in New Orleans, the sisters set about founding schools and orphanages, ministering to the poor and providing much-needed medical care that stemmed the

The Ursuline Convent is the oldest building in the Mississippi River Valley.

rampant tide of disease in the fetid environment. Miraculously, the fortlike convent did not fall to the 1788 fire, but survived to house the archives of the archdiocese, as well as dozens of oil paintings, religious statues, busts, and much of its original architecture. 1110 Chartres Street, at Ursulines Street, (504) 529-3040. Tours Tues–Fri at 10, 11, 1, 2, 3; weekends at 11:15, 1, 2. Adults $5, seniors $4, students/children $2. FRENCH QUARTER

8. Lafitte's Blacksmith Shop. Built sometime before 1772 as a legitimate-looking enterprise that disguised the smuggling operations of privateer Jean Lafitte, this candlelit space at the corner of Bourbon and St. Phillip Streets may be the oldest continually operating bar in the country, and it serves as one of the best remaining examples of French colonial architecture left in the Quarter. This unassuming little tavern fills with locals on most evenings, and features an intimate piano bar where you may hear some of the myriad songs about New Orleans, from "St. James Infirmary Blues" to "House of the Rising Sun." 941 Bourbon Street, (504) 593-9761. As with all the bars in the French Quarter, this one is open 20–23 hours per day. FRENCH QUARTER

Lafitte's Blacksmith Shop is now a tavern that's popular with the locals.

9. Congo Square, in Louis Armstrong Park. On eighteenth-century Sundays, black slaves would congregate here to play music, dance, and hold a public market, earning money from selling craft items and other wares in hopes of buying their freedom. Brass bands began to perform here in the mid- to late-1800s, and later Congo Square and Armstrong Park became the original site of the New Orleans Jazz & Heritage Festival (now moved to New Orleans Fairgrounds). Today, brass band parades, protest marches, drum circles, and gospel festivals still make this a lively area. **Louis Armstrong Park,** North Rampart Street, between St. Philip and Basin Streets, (504) 658-2299, www.nps.gov/archive/jazz/ Armstrong%20Park.htm. Open 24/7. Free. TREMÉ

Slaves gathered in Congo Square every Sunday to sing, dance, and hold a public market.

St. Louis Cemetery No. 1 is the oldest of the "cities of the dead."

10. St. Louis Cemetery No. 1. The oldest and best known of New Orleans' "cities of the dead," this graveyard filled with above-ground tombs was founded in 1789 and is one of the most iconic sights in the city. Voodoo queen Marie Laveau rests here in Tomb 347, as does plantation owner Bernard Marigny—and this is where the famous acid-trip scene in *Easy Rider* was shot. You will hear two different stories about why these cemeteries are built above ground: The myth is that the water table forces buried bodies to the surface—and while this does take place, it's not the reason for the tall tombs. In truth, the tombs actually follow the Latin custom, prevalent in Rome and other European cities, of interring the dead in these mausoleum-like structures. 420 Basin Street between Conti and St. Louis Streets, (504) 596-3050, www.saveourcemeteries.org. Mon–Sat 9–3, Sun 9 a.m.–12 p.m., closed some holidays. TREMÉ

11. Pitot House. The former residence of New Orleans' first mayor, James Pitot, this eighteenth-century Creole colonial house features brick-between-post construction, a double-pitched hipped roof, and stucco coating. This is the only house of this style in New Orleans that offers tours, giving you a rare opportunity to see what Creole architecture is all about. 1440 Moss Street, (504) 482-0312, www.pitothouse.org. Wed–Sat 10–3 (call ahead to verify). Adults $5, children and seniors $3, children under 8 free. MID-CITY

The Pitot House is an excellent example of Creole Colonial architecture.

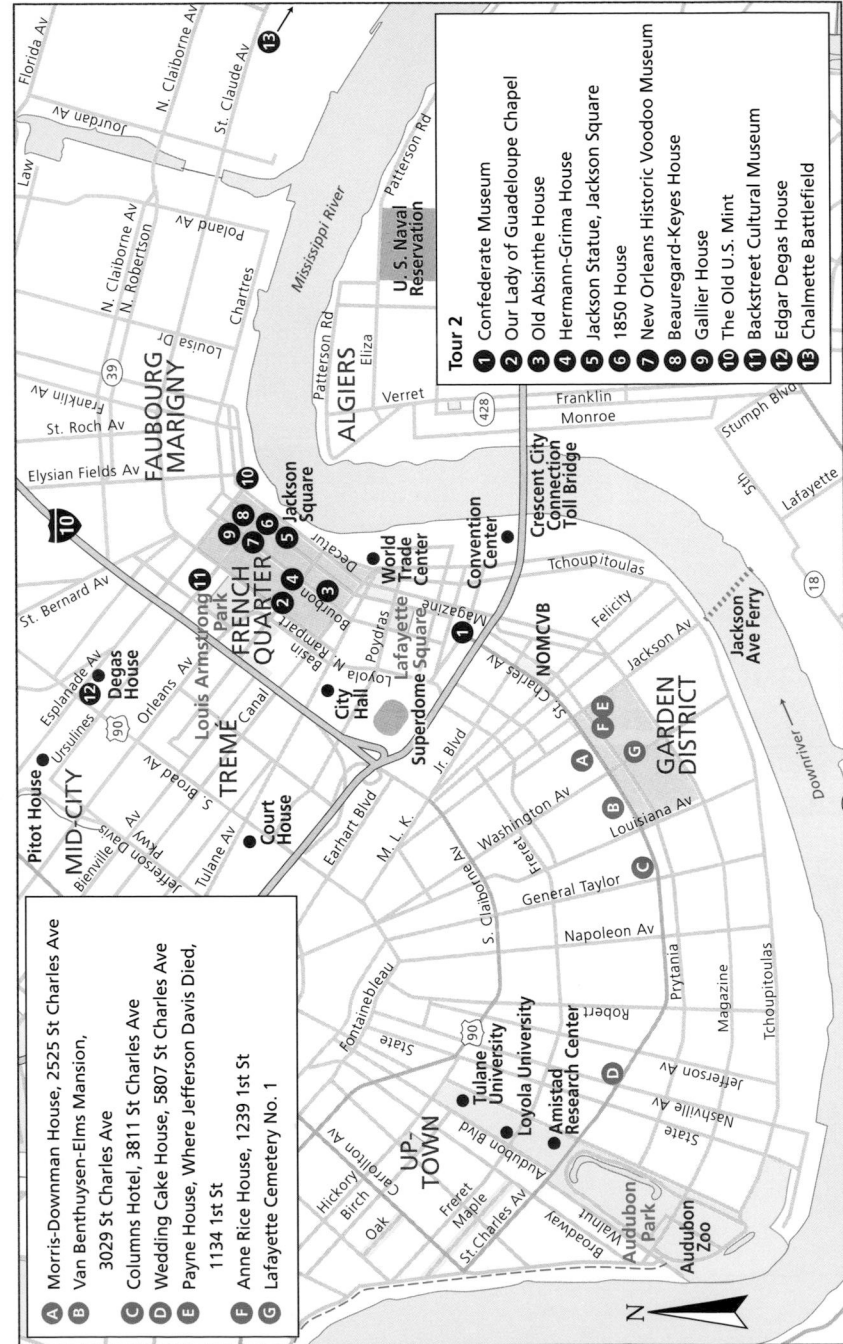

New Orleans

Tour 2

1. Confederate Museum
2. Our Lady of Guadeloupe Chapel
3. Old Absinthe House
4. Hermann-Grima House
5. Jackson Statue, Jackson Square
6. 1850 House
7. New Orleans Historic Voodoo Museum
8. Beauregard-Keyes House
9. Gallier House
10. The Old U.S. Mint
11. Backstreet Cultural Museum
12. Edgar Degas House
13. Chalmette Battlefield

A. Morris-Downman House, 2525 St Charles Ave
B. Van Benthuysen-Elms Mansion, 3029 St Charles Ave
C. Columns Hotel, 3811 St Charles Ave
D. Wedding Cake House, 5807 St Charles Ave
E. Payne House, Where Jefferson Davis Died, 1134 1st St
F. Anne Rice House, 1239 1st St
G. Lafayette Cemetery No. 1

Tour 2: 1803–1900
War, Peace, and Prosperity
in the Delta

Now a property of the United States, the territory just north of the Mississippi Delta entered a
period of prosperity bolstered by political stability.
Wealthy landowners in and around the city of New
Orleans began to look carefully at how they might
benefit from becoming part of the new country,
while new leadership examined options that would
strengthen the city's position as an important port
on the mighty river.

In 1783 Claude Tremé, a real estate developer
from Sauvigny, a town in the French province of
Burgundy, purchased the Morand Plantation and
the adjoining land on which two forts stood. Tremé
owned this land for barely a decade, but the development that grew here after he sold the property
still bears his name more than two hundred years
later. Just across North Rampart Street from the
French Quarter, Faubourg Tremé (or Tremé for
short) became a neighborhood populated primary
by free people of color.

Another plantation owner left an equally indelible
imprint on the city: Bernard Xavier Phillipe de Marigny, a roué with a nagging gambling habit, became
the heir of the grand Fontainebleau plantation in the
French Quarter. Beleaguered by gambling debts he
acquired during a tour of Europe, Marigny carved
up his land into fractional parcels and sold them
off one by one, creating a neighborhood of small
houses on small plots and lending his name to the
development. Faubourg Marigny today provides

homes to nearly two thousand families, and its Frenchman Street remains one of the city's best-known centers for live music and ethnic food.

New Orleans' first mayor, Etienne de Boré, lasted just a year in the post before resigning to tend to his business affairs. French-born nobleman James Pitot, a city council member and prosperous merchant, took on the responsibility of leading the city into its next phase: With its strategically advantageous location just a few miles north of the Mississippi River's junction with the Gulf of Mexico, New Orleans had the opportunity to become a major power in the southern United States—if its internal waterways could be strengthened to accommodate the largest ships.

Pitot set the Orleans Navigation Company to the task of improving the Carondelet Canal, a 1.6-mile water lane from Bayou St. John to an 80,000-square-foot turning basin. Originally built in 1794, the canal received an 1805 makeover that made it deeper and wider, turning it into an important shipping lane to Lake Pontchartrain.

Statehood in Time for War

On April 30, 1812, Louisiana became the nation's eighteenth state just six weeks before the United States declared war on Britain. The War of 1812 began as a battle against British policies that restrained U.S. trade with other European nations, and against the illegal British practice of impressing American men into service in the British navy.

Even with war on the horizon, however, New Orleans continued to thrive as a flourishing port city in a brand-new state. The year 1812 saw the first steamboats arrive in New Orleans, and with the travel and shipping time drastically reduced by steam power, farmers and merchants could sell their goods in New Orleans and return to the northern territories in a matter of days instead of weeks or months. A new era of commerce and enterprise came down the river into New Orleans, swelling the city's population and bringing employment and prosperity to its residents.

When representatives of the United States and Britain signed the Treaty of Ghent in the Netherlands on December 24, 1814, bringing the War of 1812 to an end, it looked like New Orleans would slip through the conflict unscathed . . . but early-nineteenth-century communications channels took weeks to get word from one side of the ocean to the other. Just two weeks later on January 8, 1815, with no information about a treaty in hand, General Andrew Jackson faced an invading British force a few miles east of New Orleans on the Chalmette

General Andrew Jackson led the U.S. to victory in the Battle of New Orleans.

The Battle of New Orleans took place on January 8, 1815.

Plantation. Many historians consider the Battle of New Orleans America's greatest land victory of the war—even though the American forces were little more than a pickup army of frontiersmen, pirates, slaves, free men of color, and men of genteel society. The battle might have ranked as a pivotal win for the Americans, if the war were not already over by the time it was fought.

With Peace Comes Commerce

As steamboats replaced other means of transporting goods and passengers, New Orleans entered a boom era loaded with commercial growth. Its population swelled to more than 40,000 residents, many of them white Americans arriving to take advantage of the new opportunities to seek their fortunes in the exotic city. Before long, friction between the white newcomers and the established French Creole residents split the city into segregated neighborhoods, with the French Quarter as the Creole bastion and an American section known as "Uptown" drawing the white residents. Canal Street became the dividing line between new and old, modern and traditional—a boundary that still stands today.

More than a thousand steamboats per year docked in New Orleans, shipping half a million bales of cotton annually. By 1840, the city was considered the second most important port in the nation, bested only by New York City. Merchants and importers congregated in New Orleans, doubling its population to 80,000 as its list of commodity products grew to include sugar, coffee, bananas, and indigo.

While the traditional Roman Catholic populace

In the 1840s, New Orleans became a leading port for the export of cotton.

had long since become integrated with people of every Western faith, one Catholic tradition hung on more strongly than others. In 1830, the rich plantation owner Marigny set about using his influence to raise money for an official Mardi Gras celebration. The traditional observance of Fat Tuesday—the day before Ash Wednesday, which signifies the beginning of Lent—had taken place in New Orleans as far back as the early 1700s, but an official event with civic sponsorship and involvement had not yet come to pass in 1830. Marigny succeeded in creating a citywide celebration. By 1838, parades on Fat Tuesday involved decorated carriages, masks, and public and private balls with lavish costumes and disguises. Each year's celebration became more raucous than the last, however, and drunken violence began to overshadow the festivities. The future of Mardi Gras grew darker and less appealing with each passing year.

Mardi Gras had already become a showy celebration by the 1830s.

Meanwhile, in the city of Mobile, Alabama, in the early morning hours of January 1, 1830, a group of young men on their way home from a New Year's party got an idea: They absconded with some display items from a store in town—including some cowbells and rakes—and demonstrated their enthusiasm for the holiday in front of the mayor's home. The mayor, clearly an enlightened gentleman, calmed the revelers down and kept them at his home until they were sober. As the young men regained their senses, the mayor suggested that they organize their celebration for the next New Year's Eve, creating an event that the public could enjoy.

The motley krewe became the Cowbellion de Rakin Society, and the parade they put together

With the Mistick Krewe of Comus in charge, Mardi Gras became fun again.

New Orleans

"It was Comus, who, in 1857, saved and transformed the dying flame of the old Creole Carnival with his enchanter's cup; it was Comus who introduced torch lit processions and thematic floats to Mardi Gras; and it was Comus who ritually closed, and still closes, the most cherished festivities of New Orleans with splendor and pomp."
—**Henri Schindler, Mardi Gras Treasures: Invitations of the Golden Age**

twelve months later became so popular that they repeated the event year after year, for the next twenty-six years. By 1856, six of their ranks had moved to New Orleans . . . and when the city announced plans to cancel Mardi Gras and end the drunken violence once and for all, the Cowbellions stepped up with an alternative plan. They proposed the creation of a private organization that would present a themed parade, a grand affair with floats, costumes, masks, and all of the positive traditions of Mardi Gras. City leaders agreed, and the club took the name of the Greek god of festivities: Comus, adding "krewe" to give themselves an air of secrecy and mystery. Comus Krewe—now the Mistick Krewe of Comus—is widely credited with saving New Orleans Mardi Gras from potential extinction and turning it into the world-famous festival that draws millions of people every February.

The Rise and Fall of New Orleans

As prosperity swelled in the Crescent City, white Americans moved down the Mississippi in droves to build spectacular mansions with palatial gardens in the city of Lafayette. The resident Creoles regarded these ostentatiously wealthy families as gauche, naming their area the "Garden District" as an insult that reflected their disdain for front-yard gardens (which they considered brazen) and opulent homes. Despite the clash between these two cultures, Lafayette became part of New Orleans, and the double-edged Garden District moniker stuck. Today bus tours bring tourists to see the majestic homes the Creoles held in such disregard.

By 1860 the annual trade in New Orleans topped $324 million, with 35,000 steamboats docking in the city's port that year alone. By this time, New Orleans' population had more than doubled to 168,000, making this the sixth largest city in America.

Wealthy merchants and business magnates built mansions on St. Charles Avenue.

Union General Benjamin Butler took control of New Orleans in 1862.

New Orleans

Satirists portray the results of General Order No. 28.

The following year, a shot rang out at Fort Sumter in South Carolina and the Civil War began in earnest, bringing the southern states' runaway prosperity to a sudden and bitter end. Louisiana seceded from the United States and became one of the Confederate States of America, while the Union set its sites on capturing the Mississippi River and holding this critical shipping lane open for the United States, simultaneously crippling the Confederacy by cutting off its strongest supply line.

That plan came to fruition early in the war. On April 18, 1862, the Union Navy attacked Forts Jackson and St. Phillip, two Confederate strongholds at the mouth of the Mississippi south of New Orleans. The Union bombarded the two forts for five days with little luck, but at 3 a.m. on April 24, Union Flag Officer David Farragut led the federal ships past the forts under cover of darkness, taking enemy firing but suffering little damage and losing only one ship. From here, it was clear sailing to New Orleans, where Farragut found the city defenseless and demanded its surrender. New Orleans was officially captured on May 1, 1862.

The Union army moved into New Orleans and occupied the city, with General Benjamin Franklin Butler in command. As often happens in wartime, the victorious force implemented harsh rule over its quarry—and while historians credit Butler with a massive cleanup effort that prevented diseases caused by sewage, dirty water, and garbage, they also acknowledge the many offenses he engineered during his command. Most notorious was General Order No. 28, which stated that any women who insulted any officer of the United States would be locked up as a prostitute.

"Passed the scene of action the City Hall, & all flashed across me. The Square is still occupied by some [Union soldiers] & there are a few remaining tents there. But the St. Charles [Hotel]! My heart sank within me when I beheld it. Never in connection with the Yankees have I experienced such sensations. It looks to be a perfect wreck. They are loitering around it, lying down, playing cards, & their clothes hanging around. Oh! it was a loathsome sight, & I wondered how men could submit to it. I couldn't . . . Saw stragglers on my way to Canal St. & there saw more, who are strutting along with such an air of defiance as I never saw, so scornful, so unassuming. Their looks being, "We have conquered you." They were sporting uniforms with any quantity of brass buttons. Oh! that our streets should be ever disgraced."
—**Clara Solomon, New Orleans resident, May 8, 1862**

Butler—nicknamed "Beast" by New Orleans residents—came under fire from both the Southern and Northern sides of the war for this behavior, and the Union saw fit to remove him from command of the Department of the Gulf in December 1862.

The war came to an end in 1865, but the return to peace did not bring prosperity back to New Orleans. The plantations farther up the Mississippi that had shipped cotton and other commodities through the Port of New Orleans lay in shambles, destroyed by the ravages of war and the lack of slave labor. The port stood in comparative silence, the steamboats nowhere to be seen as the city tumbled into a period of want.

Because of the high percentage of free people of color living in the city before and during the war—many of them from the Caribbean islands as well as Africa—New Orleans had always enjoyed a more tolerant society than many other southern cities. This came to an end with a crash in 1866, with a deadly demonstration of racial hatred during a State Constitutional Convention at Mechanics Hall on July 30.

A riot broke out at the state convention in 1866.

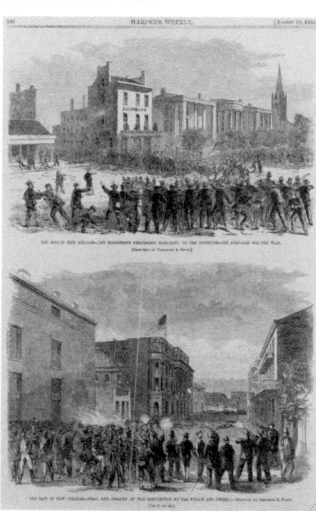

On the meeting's agenda was the enactment of new legislation that would give black men full rights as citizens, including the ability to vote. Before the vote could take place, however, the meeting dissolved into an ugly riot, with blazing firearms and hand-to-hand combat, leaving thirty-four African-American delegates and three white delegates dead, and wounding 136 others. The massacre signaled the escalation of a reign of terror against the newly freed citizens.

In 1874, with Reconstruction well underway in the South, a group of Louisiana Democrats came together to resist the changes taking place throughout the state. The White League, which described itself as the military arm of the Democratic Party, operated openly and sought public support for its method of operation. The group's deeds included the Coushatta Massacre of 1874, in which they forced six Republican legislators in the seat of Red River Parish, Louisiana, to resign from their posts at gunpoint and sign a statement saying they would leave the state—and then assassinated them before they could carry out their oath.

In New Orleans, the White League faced off with the Republican integrated police force in the French Quarter on September 14, 1874, instigating a battle that ended in the state's government leaders fleeing the capital city and a Democratic governor, John McEnery, taking his place. His term met a rapid end, however: Showing no tolerance for this kind of bloody coup, the United States government sent military troops to New Orleans and reinstated the original government three days later. Nonetheless, the White League's followers touted the temporary

The emergence of the White League brought violence and unrest.

takeover as a victory for "white supremacy," a term that would become the battle cry for generations of segregation and racial prejudice.

As trade began to increase and the old plantations found new ways to operate without slave labor, the city's former glory began to return. By 1884, nearly one-third of all the cotton produced in the United States passed through New Orleans' port.

New Orleans was home to black and white citizens in the late 1800s.

A Court Case Fuels the Race Battle

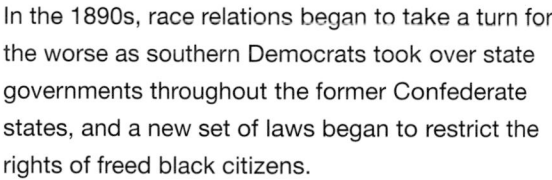

In the 1890s, race relations began to take a turn for the worse as southern Democrats took over state governments throughout the former Confederate states, and a new set of laws began to restrict the rights of freed black citizens.

Beginning in Mississippi in 1890, a series of state constitutional amendments restricted voter registration and participation in elections, prohibiting many black and poverty-level white people from voting. The requirements that voters be literate, that they live only in certain areas of each city, and that they pay poll taxes effectively disenfranchised poor citizens—many of whom were black—while denying these people the right to serve on a jury, run for office, or be heard through the electoral process. These laws became known by a name that would resonate through the nation's next seven decades: Jim Crow.

At the same time, the State of Louisiana passed an act that mandated separate railroad cars for black and white passengers. While specifying that the condition of the cars be "equal," the law raised a red flag for a group of New Orleans citizens in

Railroads had "separate but equal" cars at the turn of the 20th century.

"We consider the underlying fallacy of the plaintiff's argument to consist in the assumption that the enforced separation of the two races stamps the colored race with a badge of inferiority. If this be so, it is not by reason of anything found in the act, but solely because the colored race chooses to put that construction upon it."
—Justice Henry Billings Brown, U.S. Supreme Court, 1896

favor of integration and equal rights for all citizens. They formed the Citizens' Committee to Test the Separate Car Act and began to explore ways to get the law off the state's books.

The committee approached Homer Plessy, who was one-eighth black, to commit an act of civil disobedience. Plessy agreed to board a train, sit in a whites-only car, and refuse to leave until he was arrested. His arrest would force the issue into the courts, bringing "separate but equal" into a discussion about its constitutionality.

Homer Adolph Plessy v. The State of Louisiana brought Plessy face-to-face with Judge John Howard Ferguson, who did not see validity in the civil rights issue. Ferguson ruled that the state had the right to regulate the railroads that operated within Louisiana. Undaunted, Plessy and the Committee of Citizens took the case to the state Supreme Court, where the judges ruled against them again; they continued their legal battle by elevating the case to the U.S. Supreme Court. They presented oral arguments in the case on April 13, 1896, before eight of the nine justices on the bench . . . and in a landmark decision that would affect African-Americans across the southern states, the justices voted seven to one against Plessy. "Separate but equal" would continue to stand on the state level until President Lyndon Johnson signed the Civil Rights Act of 1964.

"Shame to Him Who Evil Thinks"

No matter where the financial condition of New Orleans stood at any time in its history, one profession always remained profitable: prostitution. Brothels were commonplace in the Crescent City, so much so that the city's government determined that the best way to contain and monitor these establishments was to create a district in which the world's oldest profession would be legal.

City Alderman Sidney Story became the leading sponsor of a bill to designate a thirty-eight-block area between Iberville, Basin, Robertson, and St. Louis Streets as New Orleans' official red-light district. In 1897, this area of town became known as Storyville, and the city published guides known as blue books that detailed the wares of each house of ill repute, describing the women within and the services they were willing to provide. On the cover of each book was the slogan *Honi Soit Qui Mal y Pense* (Shame to Him Who Evil Thinks).

Predictably, Storyville—known to the locals simply as the District—became exceedingly popular with New Orleans residents and visitors. Standing adjacent to the Basin Street railway station, Storyville was easy to reach, and no questions were asked once a patron arrived. Even black men, who were officially prohibited from enjoying the

Basin Street Station is all that remains of Storyville.

District's women, attended brothels in which black women were only too happy to serve their needs, while police and government officials turned a purposeful blind eye.

Behind screens in the parlors of these bawdy houses, a crop of supremely talented musicians gave voice to a new form of music. Blending elements of complex African rhythms, Caribbean syncopation, military brass bands, and gospel, this new music—called "jazz," a slang term for sex—began to capture the imaginations and the hearts of those who danced to its rhythms in the front rooms of Storyville's most popular bordellos. The likes of Jelly Roll Morton, Buddy Bolden, Sidney Bechet, Freddie Keppard, Manuel Perez, Kid Ory, and many others got their first audiences behind those screens, providing music to revelers as they sought life's legal pleasures in the heart of the Crescent City.

Begin your tour in the Warehouse District at the Confederate Museum, by taking the St. Charles Avenue streetcar to Lee Circle and walking east from the stop to Camp Street. To proceed after the museum, take the St. Charles streetcar to the end of its line at Canal Street, and walk west on Canal to Rampart Street. Turn right on Rampart and continue to Our Lady of Guadalupe Church.

1. Confederate Museum. This is the place to see as many as a thousand artifacts and memorabilia of the Civil War, including many items from this museum's portion of the Jefferson Davis Collection. See uniforms, weapons, and items from everyday army life, including the personal property of several Confederate generals, including Robert E. Lee. 929 Camp Street, (504) 523-4522, www .confederatemuseum.com. Wed–Sat 10–4. Adults $7, seniors, students, and active military $5, ages 12 and under $2.

The Confederate Museum is adjacent to the Ogden Museum of Southern Art.

St. Jude stands watch beside Our Lady of Guadalupe Chapel.

2. Our Lady of Guadeloupe Chapel/International Shrine of St. Jude. Built as a funeral chapel in 1826 for St. Louis Cemetery No. 1, this church—originally named the Chapel of Saint Anthony of Padua—provided services at the burials of yellow fever victims. Today it stands as the oldest church building in New Orleans and the home of a shrine to St. Jude, founded by parishioners who prayed to the saint in the 1930s and received the answers they sought. Don't miss the statue of Saint Expedite, which got its name from the crate in which it was delivered (this is not a joke). 411 North Rampart Street, (504) 525-1551. Daily 9–5. Free. FRENCH QUARTER

New Orleans

The Absinthe House Frappe is a New Orleans favorite.

3. Old Absinthe House. Originally an importing firm and later a corner grocery, this circa-1815 bar has hosted such luminaries as Oscar Wilde, Sarah Bernhardt, Walt Whitman, and Andrew Jackson; not to mention Jean Lafitte and his brother and fellow smuggler, Pierre. Today a discerning clientele stops in for the Absinthe House Frappe—a licorice-flavored, ice-laden cocktail invented here in 1874. Though the original, supposedly hallucinogenic absinthe was banned in the U.S. for close to a hundred years, the ban was lifted (with some stipulations) in 2007 and you now have your choice of six different distillations of the brew for your frappe. 240 Bourbon Street, (504) 523-3181, www.oldabsinthehouse.com. Sun–Thurs 9:30 a.m.–2 a.m., Fri–Sat 9:30 a.m.–4 a.m. FRENCH QUARTER

4. Hermann-Grima House. A Federal mansion with the only functioning outdoor kitchen in the French Quarter, this former home of two Creole families—the Hermanns and the Grimas—received a meticulous restoration to remind us of the wealthy lifestyle they enjoyed during the period from 1831 to 1860. Built for Samuel Hermann in 1831, the house was purchased by Felix Grima, a judge and notary public, in 1844, and stayed in the Grima family through 1921. Some furnishings are original to the house. 820 St. Louis Street, (504) 525-5661, www.hgghh.org. Mon, Tues, Thurs, and Fri on the hour 10–3; Wed by appointment only; Sat on the hour 12–3. Adults $10, seniors, students, AAA members, and children ages 8–18 $8, children under 8 free. With Gallier House: adults $18, seniors, students, AAA members, and children ages 8–18 $15, children under 8 free. FRENCH QUARTER

The Hermann-Grima House still has its 1830s outdoor kitchen.

5. General Andrew Jackson Statue, Jackson Square. Sculpted in the 1850s by American artist Clark Mills, this statue ostensibly was created to please the Baroness Micaela Almonester de Pontalba, who financed the formal gardens and pathways we can enjoy here today. The baroness also ordered and paid for the 1848 construction of the Upper and Lower Pontalba apartment buildings that flank the square. Come for the statue, but stay for the musicians, artists, and hawkers who offer their wares in this sunny square just a block from the river. Between Chartres and Decatur Streets to the east and west, and St. Ann and St. Peter Streets to the north and south. FRENCH QUARTER

General Jackson doffs his hat in the square that bears his name.

6. 1850 House/Louisiana State Museum. This carefully preserved building's construction was ordered in 1850 by the Baroness de Pontalba, daughter of Don Andrés Almonester y Roxas, a Spanish colonial landowner who also built the Cabildo, Cathedral, and Presbytère. The museum houses a collection of thousands of artifacts that reflect the state's history through visual arts, costumes, and textiles, science and technology, jazz, and historical context. The 1850 House, next door to the museum, showcases the elegant tastes of Baroness Pontalba during her residency in the antebellum era. Lower Pontalba Building, 523 St. Ann Street, (504) 568-6968, http://lsm.crt.state.la.us. Tues, Wed, Fri 9–3:30, Thurs 9–8, Sat 9–4:30, Sun 1–4:30; closed Monday and major holidays. Free. FRENCH QUARTER

Learn the truth about voodoo at the museum on Dumaine Street.

7. New Orleans Historic Voodoo Museum. As Creoles became a culture of their own, the unique blend of voodoo influences associated with New Orleans took shape. This shadowy, eerie museum is the only place in the city to learn how voodoo, Mardi Gras, African spirits, and Catholic saints all came together in one place. Learn about the real meaning of voodoo dolls (used in healing, not for torture), the use of juju (amulets and charms) in doorways to ward evil spirits away from the home, and the ways in which many Africans substituted the names of Catholic saints for Zombi, Rougarou, and other Senegambian gods to fool their masters into believing they had converted. 724 Dumaine Street, (504) 680-0128, www.voodoomuseum.com. Daily 10–6:30. $5. FRENCH QUARTER

8. Beauregard-Keyes House. This raised center hall house was named for two former tenants: General P.G.T. Beauregard of the Confederate States of America, who ordered the first shot of the Civil War fired at Fort Sumter; and author Frances Parkinson Keyes, who used the home as her winter residence for twenty-five years. Some rooms have their original furnishings; don't miss Mrs. Keyes' collection of more than 200 antique dolls. 1113 Chartres Street, (504) 523-7257, www .bkhouse.org. Mon–Sat 10–3. Adults $5, seniors and students $4, ages 6–12 $2, children under 6 free. FRENCH QUARTER

Take a tour of the Beauregard-Keyes House.

9. Gallier House. Built by one of New Orleans most celebrated architects, James Gallier, this house has been carefully restored with furniture and decoration that showcase its tasteful opulence. Come in summer to see it in "summer dress," a New Orleans custom of replacing heavy drapes and fabrics with linens and grass mats. 1132 Royal Street, (504) 525-5661, www.hgghh .org. Mon, Tues, Thurs, and Fri on the hour 10–3; Wed by appointment only; Sat on the hour 12–3. Adults $10, seniors, students, AAA members, and children ages 8–18 $8, children under 8 free. With Hermann-Grima House: adults $18, seniors, students, AAA members, and children ages 8–18 $15, children under 8 free. FRENCH QUARTER

Gallier House features distinctive green grillwork.

10. Old U.S. Mint. The only building in America to have served as both a U.S. and Confederate mint, this money factory originated as the idea of President Andrew Jackson, to help finance the country's western expansion. Designed in the

The original equipment for coinmaking remains at the Old U.S. Mint.

Greek Revival style, it served as a mint from 1835 through 1909. Now part of the Louisiana State Museum, the mint's exhibits will delight numismatists: The first floor contains the equipment used to manufacture coins in the nineteenth century, as well as a selection of some of the most famous and valuable coins created in this building. The second floor serves as a museum of jazz history. 400 Esplanade Street, (504) 568-4995, http://lsm .crt.state.la.us. Tues–Sun 10–4:30; closed Monday and major holidays. Adults $5, seniors, students, and active military $4, children under 12 free. FRENCH QUARTER

11. Backstreet Cultural Museum. There's no better place in New Orleans to get a close look at the costumes of Mardi Gras Indians, the men and women of color who perform in the holiday parades in Tremé. Flamboyantly beaded by hand, these extravagantly decorated suits of feathers, stays, and sequins are worn in just one Mardi Gras celebration, and then donated to the museum. The museum is also a leading source of information on jazz funerals and the tradition of Second Line, and

New Orleans

Get close looks at costumes for the Mardi Gras Indians at the Backstreet Cultural Museum.

on the Social Aid and Pleasure Clubs that come together to honor the dead and celebrate the living. This little museum is really a treat. 1116 St. Claude Avenue, (504) 303-9058, www.backstreetmuseum .org. Tues–Sat 10–5. $8. TREMÉ

12. Edgar Degas House. Master French Impressionist painter Edgar Degas lived here for four-and-a-half months in 1872 and 1873, and painted eighteen works in his New Orleans series here. Degas credited his time in New Orleans with his first venture into the impressionist style. His mother's family lived here when the home was built in 1852, and an aunt, uncle, and several cousins were among the eighteen people, including boarders, who inhabited the double house during Degas' visit. 2306 Esplanade Avenue, (504) 821-5009, www.degashouse.com. Tours by appointment only. Adults $10, seniors $8, children 5 and older and students $5. MID-CITY

Edgar Degas painted his first Impressionist works in this house.

13. Chalmette Battlefield and National Cemetery. This is the site of the January 1815 Battle of New Orleans—a preserved open field overlooking the Mississippi River. See the film in the visitor center, tour the national cemetery where Louisiana's Civil War soldiers are buried, and walk the battlefield to the Chalmette Monument and the reconstructed earthen rampart that kept the American soldiers safe from British gun and cannon fire. 8606 West St. Bernard Highway, Chalmette (a 20-minute drive from New Orleans), (504) 281-0511, www.nps.gov/jela/chalmette-battlefield.htm. Daily 9–4:30; closed Mardi Gras and Christmas. CHALMETTE

A lone monument stands on the site of the Battle of New Orleans.

A Streetcar Named St. Charles: See the Grand Mansions of New Orleans

Ride the historic St. Charles Streetcar for just $1.25.

In its most prosperous days during the 1850s, and while the Crescent City enjoyed a post-Reconstruction renaissance at the turn of the twentieth century, New Orleans became the most desirable place for the South's wealthiest citizens to build their dream homes. Today we can enjoy a ride along one of America's most impressive boulevards to view these spectacular mansions and marvel at their superb representations of Greek Revival, Mediterranean, and Creole architectural styles.

For just $1.25 in each direction (or for a $5 day pass, which gives you all the on-and-off privileges you want for a single day), you'll ride St. Charles Avenue in style aboard one of New Orleans' historic green streetcars. Board the car at the stop at the corner of St. Charles Avenue and Canal Street; the streetcar enters the Garden District at Lee Circle and continues about 13 miles to the end of the line in Carrolton—about a forty-five-minute ride.

The Van Benthuysen-Elms Mansion was the home of a Confederate veteran and streetcar magnate.

Along the way, watch for some of the avenue's most distinctive homes:

The Morris-Downman House (2525), built in 1888 as a residence of the John A. Morris family—a founder of the Louisiana State Lottery Company, and later the home of Robert Henry Downman, who became Rex, King of the Carnival, in the 1907 Mardi Gras celebration.

The Van Benthuysen-Elms Mansion (3029), the former home of Captain Watson Van Benthuysen II, a Confederate Army veteran who owned shares in the New Orleans streetcar line. From 1931 to 1941, it became the German Consulate General, from which a German captain informed Axis submarines of ship departures from the New Orleans ports.

The Columns (3811), former home of the largest cigar manufacturer in the country and later a boarding house, where the film *Pretty Baby* was shot in 1982; today it's a posh hotel.

The Victorian-revival mansion at 5807, nicknamed the **Wedding Cake House,** an extraordinary home liberally detailed with the frills and furbelows that we usually see created in frosting.

You may want to get off at 1st Street and walk down St. Charles to have more time to enjoy the architecture. A few quick detours down the numbered streets will bring you to several particular points of interest:

Jefferson Davis, president of the Confederate States of America, died in the **Payne House** at 1134 1st Street on December 6, 1889. Davis was eighty-one at the time of his passing, and his funeral several days later in Richmond, Virginia, remains one of the largest ever seen in the southern states.

Look for the historical marker to find Payne House, where Confederacy president Jefferson Davis died in 1889.

The Wedding Cake mansion looks decorated with icing.

Best-selling author Anne Rice lived and wrote in the house at **1239 First Street** (at the corner of Chestnut Street), a home that served as the inspiration for Mayfair Manor, where her Mayfair Witches resided. It's said that Rice frequented Lafayette Cemetery No. 1, between Washington and Sixth Streets just a few blocks from this house; cemetery research director Sean Perry tells us that he often gets questions from tourists about which of the cemetery's aboveground tombs holds the Mayfair family. (The witches are not buried there. The books are fiction.)

Lafayette Cemetery No. 1 is one of the most fascinating of the "cities of the dead" in New Orleans. Lacking the financial commitment to perpetual care that more affluent citizens purchased for the scrubbed white tombs in some other cemeteries, this graveyard has had the opportunity to decay in a deliciously creepy manner—made even more interesting by the cemetery's research director, Sean Perry, who gives impromptu tours of the tombs from the inside out. Learn about the use of these tombs from the 1800s through present day, and the process through which cemetery workers clear space for the next body when another family member is added to the tomb's contents. Between Prytania, Coliseum, Washington, and Sixth Streets, (504) 452-1088, www.lafayettecemetery.org. Mon–Fri 7 a.m.–2:30 p.m., Sat 7 a.m.–12 p.m; closed Sunday except for Mother's Day, Father's Day, and All Saints Day. $10 donation requested for tour.

Tour Lafayette Cemetery No. 1 with research director Sean Perry, and you might get a look inside a tomb.

Tour 3: 1901–1950
The Big Easy Makes a
Joyful Noise

Jazz, baby! The city resounded with it at the turn
of the twentieth century, an entirely new and
uniquely American amalgamation that would turn
the national music scene on its ear. The poly-
rhythms that had reverberated through Congo
Square more than a century earlier now formed
the backbeat of an art form that resonated through
instruments made popular by military bands: the
trumpet, cornet, clarinet, and trombone. Steeped
in the call-and-response spirituals sung in farmers'
fields, and a major break from the strong bass lines
and specific chord progressions of the blues, jazz
embraces syncopation, counterpoint, and a con-
versational structure in which instruments actually
seem to communicate with one another, bouncing
the melody from one to the next as each musician demonstrates his solo prowess. Hot on the
heels of the popular ragtime piano sound of the
great Scott Joplin, whose "Maple Leaf Rag" sold
more than one million copies of sheet music and
launched a new musical genre in its own right, jazz
became the music of choice in the parlor of every
brothel in Storyville.

No one could predict the phenomenon that
began on August 4, 1901, when a boy was born
to a poor New Orleans family in the Back of
Town neighborhood. Louis Armstrong spent his
childhood hanging around the dance halls in
Storyville—particularly the Funky Butt—listening

Louis Armstrong and his horn
are immortalized in the park
that bears his name.

A Guided Tour through History

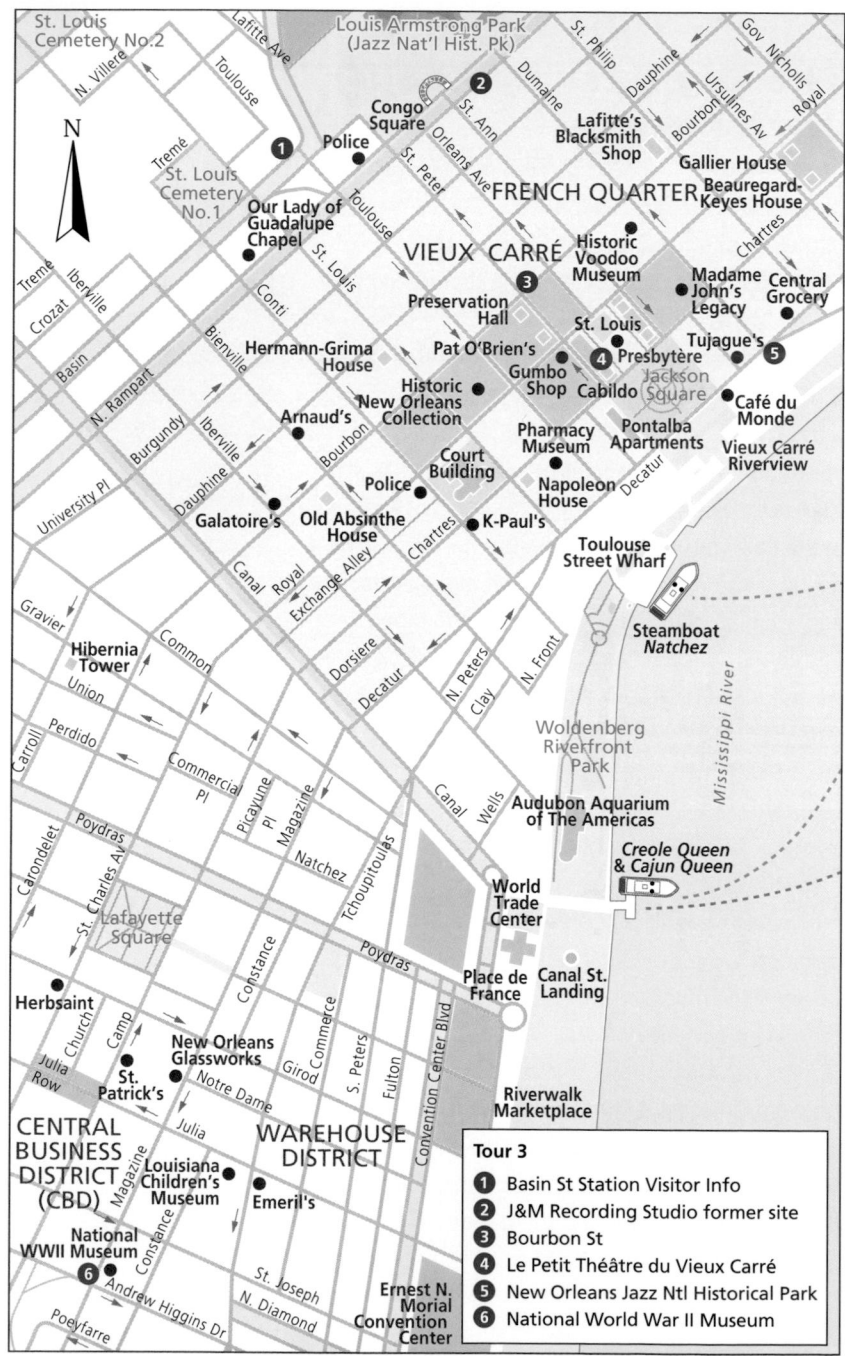

St. Louis
Cemetery No.2

Lafitte Ave

Toulouse

N. Villere

Treme

St. Louis
Cemetery
No.1

Our Lady of
Guadalupe
Chapel

Louis Armstrong Park
(Jazz Nat'l Hist. Pk)

St. Philip

Dumaine

Dauphine

Ursulines Av

Gov Nicholls

Royal

Congo
Square

St. Ann

Orleans Ave

St. Peter

Toulouse

Lafitte's
Blacksmith
Shop

Bourbon

Gallier House

Police ●

● Police ①

② ●

FRENCH QUARTER

Beauregard-
Keyes House

Treme

Iberville

Crozat

Basin

N. Rampart

Conti

Brienville

Iberville

Burgundy

St. Louis

VIEUX CARRÉ

Preservation
Hall ③

Hermann-Grima
House

Historic
New Orleans
Collection

Arnaud's

Bourbon

Pat O'Brien's

Gumbo
Shop Cabildo

Pharmacy
Museum

Court
Building

Police ●

● K-Paul's

Historic
Voodoo
Museum

Madame
● John's
Legacy

Central
Grocery

Chartres

St. Louis

Presbytère ④

Jackson
Square

Pontalba
Apartments

Napoleon
House

Decatur

Tujague's
⑤ ●

Café du
Monde

Vieux Carré
Riverview

University Pl

Dauphine

Galatoire's

Old Absinthe
House

Chartres

Canal

Royal

Exchange Alley

Chartres

Toulouse
Street Wharf

Gravier

Hibernia
Tower

Common

Union

Perdido

Carroll

Dorsiere

Decatur

N. Peters

Clay

N. Front

Steamboat
Natchez

Mississippi River

Commercial
Pl

Picayune Pl

Magazine

Poydras

Natchez

Tchoupitoulas

Canal

Wells

Woldenberg
Riverfront
Park

Audubon Aquarium
of The Americas

Carondelet

St. Charles Av

Lafayette
Square

Constance

Poydras

World
Trade
Center

Creole Queen
& Cajun Queen

Herbsaint ●

Church

Camp

Julia
Row

St.
Patrick's ●

New Orleans
Glassworks

Notre Dame

Girod

Commerce

S. Peters

Fulton

Convention Center Blvd

Place de
France

Canal St.
Landing

Riverwalk
Marketplace

CENTRAL
BUSINESS
DISTRICT
(CBD)

Magazine

Julia

Louisiana
Children's
Museum

WAREHOUSE
DISTRICT

Emeril's

National
WWII Museum

⑥ ●

Constance

Andrew Higgins Dr

St. Joseph

N. Diamond

Ernest N.
Morial
Convention
Center

Poeyfarre

Tour 3

① Basin St Station Visitor Info
② J&M Recording Studio former site
③ Bourbon St
④ Le Petit Théâtre du Vieux Carré
⑤ New Orleans Jazz Ntl Historical Park
⑥ National World War II Museum

Louis Armstrong learned jazz by growing up in New Orleans.

to the bands that played in the bordello parlors. Learning the cornet from King Oliver, Armstrong became a serious musician while playing in the band at the New Orleans Home for Colored Waifs, a juvenile home for delinquents at which he spent considerable time. By the time he was fourteen, he had already begun playing professionally at Henry Ponce's, and soon joined the brass band parades that marched through the city's streets, picking up technique from jazz greats like Bunk Johnson, Buddy Petit, Kid Ory, and his father figure and mentor, King Oliver.

Armstrong became one of the first musicians to carry jazz up the Mississippi River to St. Louis, Kansas City, and Chicago, and as his popularity grew he maintained an enormous tour schedule, often on the road for 300 days of the year. New Orleans can take credit for fostering one of the first great celebrities of the twentieth century, a groundbreaking musician and major personality who helped put jazz on the international map.

A Bigger, Drier City

Against this bed of musical themes, New Orleans worked its way out of its post–Civil War doldrums and into a new period of prosperity and growth. In this progressive era, developers began to examine the lower ground west of the French Quarter and south of Lake Pontchartrain, where the frequently flooded "back swamp" had always been considered unsuitable for housing or commercial use. A massive exploration of the issue combined the efforts of the Drainage Advisory Board and the Sewerage and Water Board of New Orleans, leading to the invention of enormous pumps by mechanical engineer and Tulane University graduate A. Baldwin Wood. The engineer's complex system of flap gates and high-volume pumps resulted in land reclaimed from the forces of nature that could now be developed. New wards and suburbs spread over this land in just a few short years. It would be decades before the city understood

New pump systems allowed New Orleans to grow.

that this former swamp continued to sink gradually below sea level, making it especially prone to
flooding during major storms.

Up, Down, and Up Again

With America's entry into the World War in 1917,
the United States Department of the Navy made
a demand of New Orleans that put an end to the
city's biggest tourist attraction. The Navy informed
the mayor of New Orleans that Storyville had to
close down, to save sailors from "temptation" (or,
perhaps, venereal disease) before they shipped out
for combat. Mayor Martin Behrman was quick to
note, "You can make it illegal, but you can't make
it unpopular."

Storyville's heyday came to an end, but the District continued to thrive throughout Prohibition as
speakeasies replaced bars, and gambling moved
to the back rooms of former brothels—in which
prostitution, despite its change in legal status,
continued to serve its regular clientele.

The World War brought another dip in New
Orleans' economy, sending it into a decline that

New Orleans saw hard times
after World War I.

would continue through the 1920s. In an effort to bolster the sagging markets, the state government authorized construction of a long-awaited deepwater canal between the Mississippi River and Lake Pontchartrain, creating jobs while opening new shipping opportunities for the beleaguered city.

When the Great Depression arrived, New Orleans went into a tailspin. By 1933, five of its local banks had failed, and eleven percent of its citizens depended on public assistance for their daily bread. The mayor at the time, T. Semmes Walmsley, entered into a bitter rivalry with Louisiana Governor Huey P. Long, launching a personal battle so vitriolic that it actually escalated into an attack by the governor on the city of New Orleans, severing state funding for the city and preventing the government from collecting taxes, regulating its utilities, and issuing licenses—all methods through which a city government funds its services to its residents.

With his city facing bankruptcy because of state policies that remained in place even after Long's assassination in 1935, Walmsley finally agreed to resign as mayor in June 1936.

Huey Long

Higgins Industries lifted the city out of the Depression.

Walmsley's eventual successor, Mayor Robert Maestri, moved quickly to embrace the funds made available through President Franklin Roosevelt's New Deal and put people to work building parks, bridges, roads, and public buildings throughout the city—and as the nation looked ahead to a possible entry into a world war in progress, New Orleans saw its next opportunity for prosperity on the horizon. By 1941, the city became a hub for shipbuilding, constructing the famous Landing Craft Vehicle Personnel boats—known colloquially as Higgins boats, in reference to their designer, Louisiana resident Andrew Higgins. The boats were used extensively in amphibious landings throughout the war and during the D-day invasion of Normandy on June 6, 1944, cementing New Orleans' place in military history.

"If Higgins had not designed and built those LCVPs, we never could have landed over an open beach. The whole strategy of the war would have been different."
—**General Dwight D. Eisenhower**

Higgins Industries left an indelible mark on New Orleans' history.

"The uptown folks thought of me as 'the n——er studio.' Even though I did people like Pete Fountain and Al Hirt, what stuck was that I worked with blacks. The studio was never in the newspaper, there were no tea dansants for me. An Italian was kind of an outcast down here, too."
—**Cosimo Matassa, owner, J&M Recording Studio**

While the city took on projects that fortified the nation's defense, a little studio in the back of a shop in Tremé made an impression on the world of metaphorically equal magnitude. An Italian immigrant's son, Cosimo Matassa began recording jazz and rhythm and blues (R & B) musicians in the back of his parents' appliance store, in a space he called J&M Recording Studio. The industry would credit his influence with the development of R & B, rock, and soul, as well as the distinctive form musicians call the New Orleans Sound—heavy guitar and bass against strong drums, coupled with light piano and horn.

Matassa recorded such classics as "The Fat Man," Fats Domino's greatest hit and one of the recordings considered to be the first example of rock 'n' roll, as well as Little Richard's "Tutti Frutti," and tracks on which major musicians including Dr. John, Allen Toussaint, Lee Dorsey, and dozens of others made their names as some of the most skilled session men in the music industry.

This building once housed J&M Recording Studio.

Begin your tour at the bend in Basin Street just south of Louis Armstrong Park, at the Basin Street Station. This is the only building that remains from the days of Storyville. From the station, walk past 838 North Rampart Street before reentering the French Quarter.

1. Basin Street Station. Formerly the New Orleans Terminal Company and the Southern Railway Freight Office Building, Basin Street Station was built to accommodate passengers on their way to Storyville, which was adjacent to this site. With Storyville's official demise in 1917, a series of urban renewal efforts swept through the area, razing the brothels and clubs and replacing them with low-income housing for the primarily black tenants, including the destruction of the original rail station here in 1956—but the freight office remained. There's a visitor center on the first floor. 501 Basin Street, corner Basin and St. Louis Streets, across from St. Louis Cemetery No. 1, (504) 293-2600, www.basinststation.com. Mon– Sun 9–5. Free. TREMÉ

2. J&M Recording Studio. It's been called "the crucible of the New Orleans sound of the 1950s," and every jazz expert knows that J&M's record- ings launched the careers of Fats Domino, Jerry Lee Lewis, Little Richard, and Ray Charles, while recording producer Cosimo Matassa worked to create the "New Orleans sound" we still recognize today. The tiny studio was in the back of this build- ing—now the Clothes Spin coin laundry—behind the Matassa family's appliance store. 838–840 North Rampart Street, at the corner of Dumaine Street. Not open to the public. TREMÉ

3. Bourbon Street. It's hard to believe to see it now, but from the late 1940s to the early 1960s, this was jazz heaven with more than a dozen clubs devoted to jazz; today only the Famous Door at 339 Bourbon and the Old Absinthe House (240 Bourbon Street) remain. Imagine Dixie's Bar of Music (no. 701, now the Cat's Meow), Pier 600 (today's Tropical Isle at no. 600), Al Hirt's Club (at no. 501, now Bourbon Vieux), 500 Club (Bourbon Street Blues, still remembering its roots at no. 441), Dream Room (no. 426, today's Jazz Emporium), Mardi Gras Lounge (Mango Mango at no. 333), Paddock Lounge (now Rick's Cabaret Gentlemen's Club at no. 315), and El Morocco (now Jester Gateway Mardi Gras at no. 200) all rocking to the music of jazz greats including Louis Armstrong, Jack Bachman, Sharkey Bonano, Len Ferguson, Pete Fountain, Al Hirt, Bob Havens, George Lewis, Steve Lewis, Lizzie Miles, Walter "Fats" Pichon, Burnell Santiago, Phil Zito, and many more. You can still hear some jazz on Bourbon Street, but it takes determination to find

It's still a party every night on Bourbon Street—but largely without jazz.

it—try Fritzel's at 733 Bourbon, and Café Beignet at Musical Legends Park, 311 Bourbon Street.
FRENCH QUARTER

4. Le Petit Théâtre du Vieux Carré. Billed as the oldest continually operating community theater in the country, Le Petit began producing shows in 1916 in the drawing room of a member's home, then moved to a rented space in the lower Pontalba Building. This Spanish-colonial-style building was constructed in 1922, rescuing this street corner from the slum it had become; today the building holds a 375-seat mainstage theater and an intimate 125-seat cabaret. 616 St. Peter Street, (504) 522-2081, www.lepetittheatre.com. Performances Thurs–Sat at 8, Sun at 2. Visit the Web site for the current production schedule and pricing.
FRENCH QUARTER

Le Petit Théâtre may be the oldest community theatre group in the country.

5. New Orleans Jazz National Historical Park. This National Park Service visitor center offers a special feature no other national park site can match: Its rangers are musicians themselves, and they offer live music performances and daily programs on the history of jazz, from Scott Joplin and Buddy Bolden to Wynton Marsalis and Harry Connick Jr. Pick up an activities calendar and schedule of concerts as you come in, or take a jazz history walking tour of the French Quarter, Faubourg Marigny, or Tremé with a park ranger as your guide. Across from the French Market, 916 North Peters Street; (504) 589-4841, (877) 520-0677; www.nps.gov/jazz. Tues–Sat 9–5; closed Thanksgiving, Christmas, New Year's Day. Free.
FRENCH QUARTER

6. National World War II Museum. New Orleans earned the honor of mounting the nation's official World War II museum because of the pivotal role the city's Higgins Industries played in Operation Overlord, the invasion of Normandy on June 6, 1944. Extensive exhibits cover that dramatic invasion as well as the D-day invasions in the Pacific, and two exclusive films provide dramatic footage of the wars in Europe and the Pacific. 945 Magazine Street, (504) 527-6012, www.nationalww2 museum.org. Daily 9–5; closed Mardi Gras, Thanksgiving, Christmas Eve, and Christmas Day. Adults $16, seniors and students $12, ages 5–12 and active or retired military and spouses $8, military in uniform and children under 5 free. WAREHOUSE DISTRICT

See a real Higgins boat at the National World War II Museum.

Tour 4: 1951–2005
The City with Nine Lives

With all of the challenges New Orleans faced in its first two centuries—changes in sovereignty, fire, war, occupation, epidemics, the Great Depression and the post-war recession—the city proved again and again that its citizens could find their way back from one slump or disaster after another.

In the latter half of the twentieth century and in 2005, the Crescent City would encounter some of the most insidious crises any metropolis could confront; yet somehow, even in the face of the most devastating hurricane of our time, New Orleans is rising from the ashes to soar once again.

The French Quarter has become one of New Orleans' greatest assets.

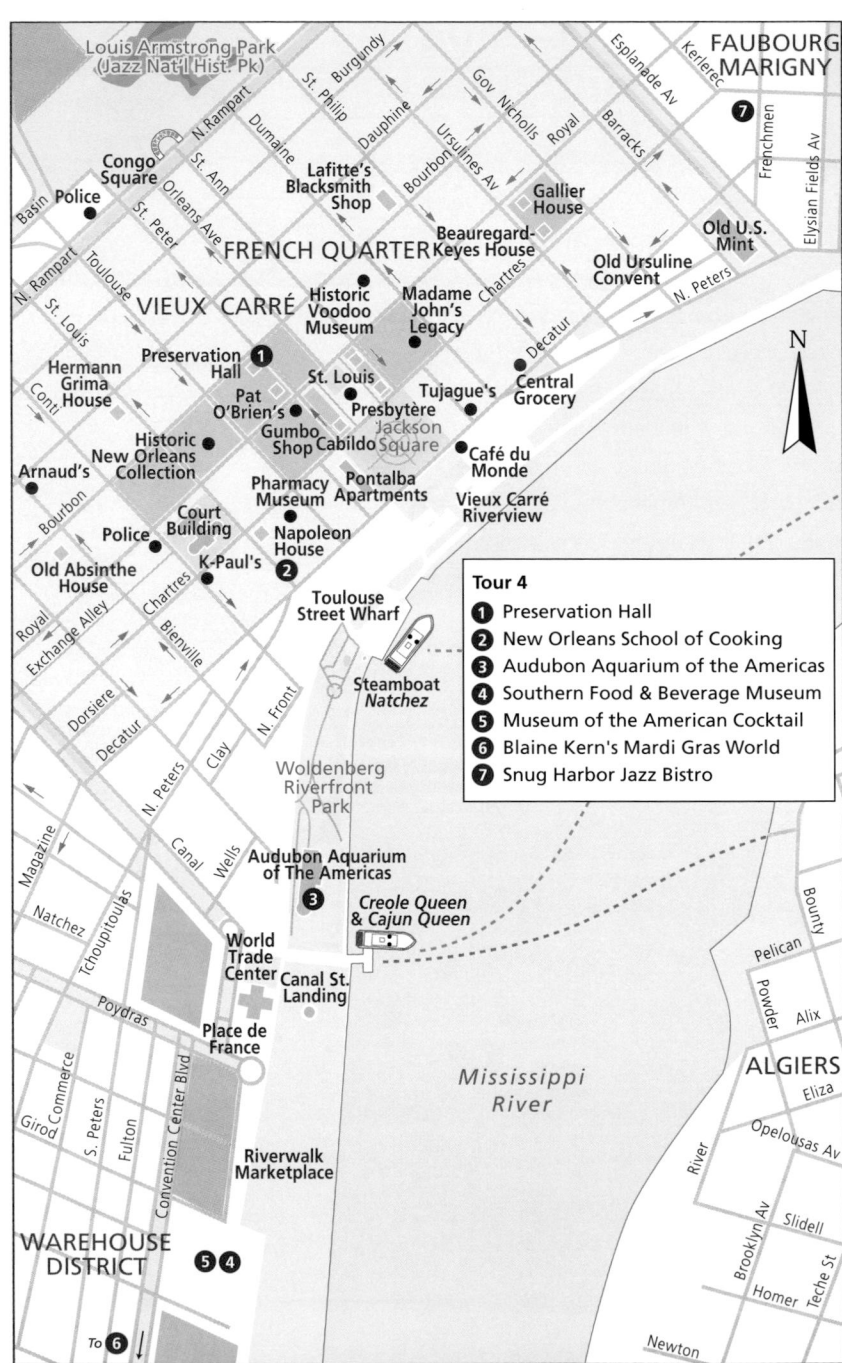

Louis Armstrong Park (Jazz Nat'l Hist. Pk)

Congo Square
Police
Basin
N. Rampart
St. Philip
Burgundy
Dumaine
St. Ann
Dauphine
Orleans Ave
St. Peter
Gov. Nicholls
Ursulines Av
Bourbon
Royal
Barracks
Esplanade Av
Kerlerec

FAUBOURG MARIGNY

Frenchmen
Elysian Fields Av

7

Lafitte's Blacksmith Shop
Gallier House
Beauregard-Keyes House
Old U.S. Mint

FRENCH QUARTER

Toulouse
N. Rampart
St. Louis
Conti

VIEUX CARRÉ

Historic Voodoo Museum
Madame John's Legacy
Old Ursuline Convent
Chartres
Decatur
N. Peters

N

Hermann Grima House
Preservation Hall **1**
St. Louis
Tujague's
Central Grocery
Pat O'Brien's
Presbytère
Jackson Square
Historic New Orleans Collection
Gumbo Shop
Cabildo
Café du Monde
Arnaud's
Bourbon
Pharmacy Museum
Pontalba Apartments
Vieux Carré Riverview
Court Building
Police
Napoleon House
K-Paul's **2**
Old Absinthe House
Chartres
Royal
Exchange Alley
Bienville
Toulouse Street Wharf

Dorsiere
Decatur
N. Peters
Clay
N. Front

Steamboat *Natchez*

Woldenberg Riverfront Park

Magazine
Natchez
Tchoupitoulas
Canal
Wells

Audubon Aquarium of The Americas

3

Creole Queen & Cajun Queen

World Trade Center
Canal St. Landing

Place de France

Poydras
Commerce
Girod
S. Peters
Fulton
Convention Center Blvd

Mississippi River

Riverwalk Marketplace

WAREHOUSE DISTRICT **5 4**

To **6**

ALGIERS

Bounty
Pelican
Powder
Alix
Eliza
Opelousas Av
River
Brooklyn Av
Slidell
Homer
Teche St
Newton

> **Tour 4**
> **1** Preservation Hall
> **2** New Orleans School of Cooking
> **3** Audubon Aquarium of the Americas
> **4** Southern Food & Beverage Museum
> **5** Museum of the American Cocktail
> **6** Blaine Kern's Mardi Gras World
> **7** Snug Harbor Jazz Bistro

A New Leader Brings a Fresh Vision

For many decades after Reconstruction, one party ran New Orleans politics: a southern Democratic regime known as the Old Regulars, most recently headed by Mayor Robert Maestri. Taking over as mayor in 1936 after the death of Governor Huey Long and the strongly encouraged resignation of Mayor T. Semmes Walmsley, Maestri took on the task of reassembling New Orleans' financial structure and reconnecting with the state, gaining back the city's ability to function and building affordable housing for many of the city's low-income families. At the same time, however, he fashioned a political machine that dispatched ward bosses into neighborhoods, extorting loyalty from citizens through intimidation.

In 1945, a young reform candidate for mayor found an easy route to the top of New Orleans civic life by vowing to reform the corruption in City Hall. DeLesseps Story Morrison, known as "Chep," handily beat Maestri in the primaries and set to work repairing the image of greed, poverty, racial unrest, and sin that pervaded the American vision of New Orleans. Morrison launched a marketing effort that reimagined New Orleans as a beautiful and exciting city, a thriving metropolis on the edge of explosive growth. He also set about making the city live up to its new reputation, engaging in "urban renewal" before the idea became popular with other large cities across the country: Morrison ordered the closing of dilapidated properties and put thousands of people to work building new housing projects and civic buildings.

The Population Boom

Across post–World War II America in the 1950s, young couples with children moved into homes of their own, sparking a construction industry boom that sent the housing industry to new heights of profitability. New Orleans enjoyed the largest years of construction in the city's history as the new Crippled Children's Hospital, extensions to Tulane and Loyola Universities, the New Orleans Civic Center, and tall office buildings shot up in the center of the city to flank the railroad's new Union Passenger Terminal. To house all the people who worked in these new facilities, developers built as many as 4,100 new homes each year, expanding the suburbs in Lakeview and Gentilly. Three new highways created fast routes from one end of the city to the other, filling in the former New Basin Canal from Rampart Street to Lake Pontchartrain and replacing it with the Pontchartrain Expressway. Soon to come was the Greater New Orleans Mississippi River Bridge, the span we now know as the Crescent City Connection—a bridge that would become the scene of a human drama that would outrage the nation in early September 2005.

New construction extended into black neighborhoods as well as white, as nearly forty percent

New Orleans

The Greater New Orleans Mississippi Bridge is one of Mayor Morrison's major accomplishments.

Protests against integration, like this one in Little Rock, Arkansas, spread across the south in 1960.

of the city's population was African-American. Morrison, however, remained a confirmed segregationist throughout his tenure as mayor—and as a result, the facilities he ordered for the urban projects became notorious for their inferior construction in comparison to similar buildings in white neighborhoods. In the fall of 1960, when the New Orleans city school board implemented the federal regulation that required integration of all schools, black children who attempted to enter white schools met walls of screaming white students and adults who hurled epithets and garbage at them—and while Morrison did nothing to prevent integration, he pointedly did nothing to stop the demonstrations and violence. With his popularity shrinking and the civil rights movement taking hold throughout New Orleans, Morrison stepped back from seeking reelection in 1962.

African Americans used the "colored only" back entrance to a movie theater in the 1960s.

The 1964 Congressional passage of the Civil Rights Act finally put an end to Jim Crow laws, and while New Orleans merchants were slow to respond, the city hosted the national meeting of the National Association for the Advancement of Colored People (NAACP) in 1965, the same year as the passage of the Voting Rights Act that forbid continuation of any tactics that prevented black citizens from voting in elections.

NASA turned to New Orleans for the construction of Saturn rocket boosters in the 1960s, one in a series of developments that signaled another boom time for the city. Downtown, the city completed construction of the World Trade Center, One Shell Square (the headquarters for Shell Oil), and a series of high-rise hotels along Canal Street. Major work began on a ship channel that allowed very large ships to enter the Port of New

Orleans, boosting the city to become the second largest port in the nation for the biggest and most powerful overseas vessels. Topping off all of these accomplishments, the National Football League awarded New Orleans a franchise, moving the New Orleans Saints into the major league.

An Island of Nostalgic Preservation

Even as downtown New Orleans shot upward and gleaming new buildings reached for the Louisiana skies, the French Quarter retained its physical links to the city's deepest roots. While most of the native Creole population moved to the suburbs and beyond, the Quarter remained an authentic experience for visitors who poured into its narrow streets year after year, attracted first by the flamboyant decadence of Mardi Gras, but compelled to wander among the rows of Spanish-inspired structures to seek their lingering sense of old world European romance.

The French Quarter retains its old world romance.

As major industries passed on making New Orleans the site of their headquarters and manufacturing operations, and the import/export business moved to a container system that eliminated the need for manual labor, tourism rose to the top of the list of the city's most effective revenue streams. Back in the 1920s and 1930s, some in city government had lobbied to tear down sections of the historic neighborhood to build low-income housing in their place, but preservationists like General Kemper Williams stepped in and bought up entire blocks of the Vieux Carré, renovating the crumbling buildings and restoring their quixotic appeal. By the 1980s, as the oil industry began

Riverwalk Marketplace provides tourists with plenty of shopping options.

to consolidate through mergers and acquisitions and many moved their headquarters out of New Orleans, little question remained that tourism had become the city's most important source of income. Soon new attractions began to appear along the Mississippi River waterfront, just across Decatur Street from the French Quarter: The old Jackson City Brewery building became a shopping and dining center, and the new Riverwalk Marketplace offered local and nationally known shops and food court options for tourists.

As the nation began to discover the hearty, spice-laden flavors of Cajun cuisine served from the kitchens of Chef Paul Prudhomme, the carefully preserved French Quarter received a year-round influx of tourists from all over the world who came to explore the subtle differences between Cajun and Creole. Mayor Ernest N. "Dutch" Morial, New Orleans' first mayor of color, seized an opportunity to focus national and even global attention on his city by hosting the 1984 New Orleans

World's Fair, the last fair of its kind in America and an attraction that brought millions of people into the city center. While the fair turned out to be a financial disaster, it did spark construction of many hotels, a convention center, and a cruise ship terminal—all boons for a city struggling to find its footing as a year-round tourism destination.

By the 1990s, when Mayor Morial's son, Marc, became one of the youngest mayors of a major city in the entire country, New Orleans had begun to enjoy another upswing. Marc Morial pushed the city to look for ways to diversify its economy, with an eye toward ending the days of dependence on one or two industries for its livelihood. Under his leadership New Orleans rose once again, recovering from the downturn in the oil industry and looking ahead to prosperity. When Clarence Ray Nagin became mayor in 2002, the future looked very bright indeed for a city that had become one of the prime tourism destinations in the United States.

1. Preservation Hall. Created to protect and honor New Orleans jazz, the unassuming hall fills to capacity every night of the week as it features jazz legends—including its own Preservation Hall Band—and young musicians and their music. You'll hear Dixieland and lots of old jazz favorites here, as the hall caters to the tourist trade, but you can't beat the quality of these fine musicians. 726 St. Peter Street, (504) 522-2841, www.preservation hall.com. Nightly 8–11 p.m., music begins at 8:15. All tickets $10.

2. The New Orleans School of Cooking and Louisiana General Store. What goes into gumbo? How do you make a roux—the key element of so

Overhead mirrors at New Orleans School of Cooking show viewers what's bubbling on the stove.

many Creole and Cajun dishes? What is the "trinity" of Louisiana cooking, and how much of it do you need? What on earth is filé? Find answers to these and dozens of other questions at this lively cooking school, where you can attend a demonstration lunch and watch a professional chef create several fragrant, hearty dishes—and then eat generous helpings of each. 524 St. Louis Street, (800) 237-4841, (504) 525-2665, www.neworleans schoolofcooking.com. Demonstration lunch daily, 10 a.m.–12:30 p.m. $27/person. Afternoon demonstration class, Fri and Sat, 2-4 p.m. FRENCH QUARTER

3. Audubon Aquarium of the Americas. One of the most popular attractions in New Orleans, the aquarium was part of the most recent thrust toward tourism along the Mississippi waterfront. The live collection at this world-class aquarium has grown once again to its pre–Hurricane Katrina splendor, making a visit to this undersea menagerie a true delight. Walk through the 30-foot-long Caribbean Reef, an aquatic tunnel filled with

132,000 gallons of water and all manner of under-water critters, or play in the Adventure Island touch tank, where you can make hand-to-fin contact with cownose rays. 1 Canal Street, at the river, (800) 774-7394, (504) 581-4629, www.audubon institute.org. Tues–Sun 10 a.m.–5 p.m. Adults $17, seniors $13, children 12 and under $10. FRENCH QUARTER

4. The Southern Food & Beverage Museum. This new museum opened in 2008, and it provides the stories of New Orleans' famous food culture, from the invention of granulated sugar to the creation of the po'boy. If you've wondered how chicory got into New Orleans coffee, who came up with the recipe for pralines, or how the snow cone was invented, you'll find all that information and more at this fun museum. Level C of Riverwalk Marketplace, 1 Poydras Street, Suite 169 (on the Julia Street side), (504) 569-0405, http://southernfood.org. Mon–Sat 10–7, Sun 12–6. Adults $10, students and seniors $5; includes admission to the Museum of the American Cocktail. WAREHOUSE DISTRICT

Learn some New Orleans food history at the Southern Food & Beverage Museum.

5. Museum of the American Cocktail. In one information-packed room, this museum traces the 9,000-year history of alcoholic beverages, starting with the earliest traces of spirits—fermented, that is—in Indian lore and whisking all the way to the sweet blender drinks of the 1980s and beyond. Many of these potions got their start here in New Orleans, including the Sazerac, which emerged at the Sazerac House Bar in the Gruenewald Hotel—now the Fairmount Hotel—as early as the 1890s. In the Southern Food & Beverage Museum, Level C of Riverwalk Marketplace, 1 Poydras Street, Suite 169, (504) 569-0405, www.museumofthe americancocktail.org. Mon–Sat 10–7, Sun 12–6. $10; includes admission to the Southern Food & Beverage Museum. WAREHOUSE DISTRICT

6. Blaine Kern's Mardi Gras World. Tour the plant in which most of the parade floats for the world's most elaborate Mardi Gras celebration are imagined, designed, and built. See Mardi Gras floats under construction, try on costumes and hats worn by parade participants, see a twelve-minute

New Orleans

Blaine Kern's Mardi Gras World takes you behind the scenes of the floatmaking industry.

movie about Mardi Gras, sample traditional king cake, and see the prop shop, where the huge figures you see in the parade are created by hand. 1380 Port of New Orleans Avenue, (504) 361-7821, www.mardigrasworld.com. Adults $18, seniors (66+), children under 12, and military $14, children under 4 free. Daily 9:30–4:30; come by 3:30 to see the prop shop in action. Closed Mardi Gras, Easter, Thanksgiving, and Christmas.

7. Snug Harbor. Off the beaten tourist path, Snug Harbor is the most reliable place in town to hear the music that made New Orleans famous, due to its dedication to presenting local jazz musicians. Nightly performances may feature young, new musicians or the likes of Ellis Marsalis—father of Branford and Wynton—or R & B vocalist Charmaine Neville. 626 Frenchmen Street, (504) 949-0696, www.snugjazz.com. Performances nightly at 8 and 10. Call for ticket prices. FAUBOURG MARIGNY

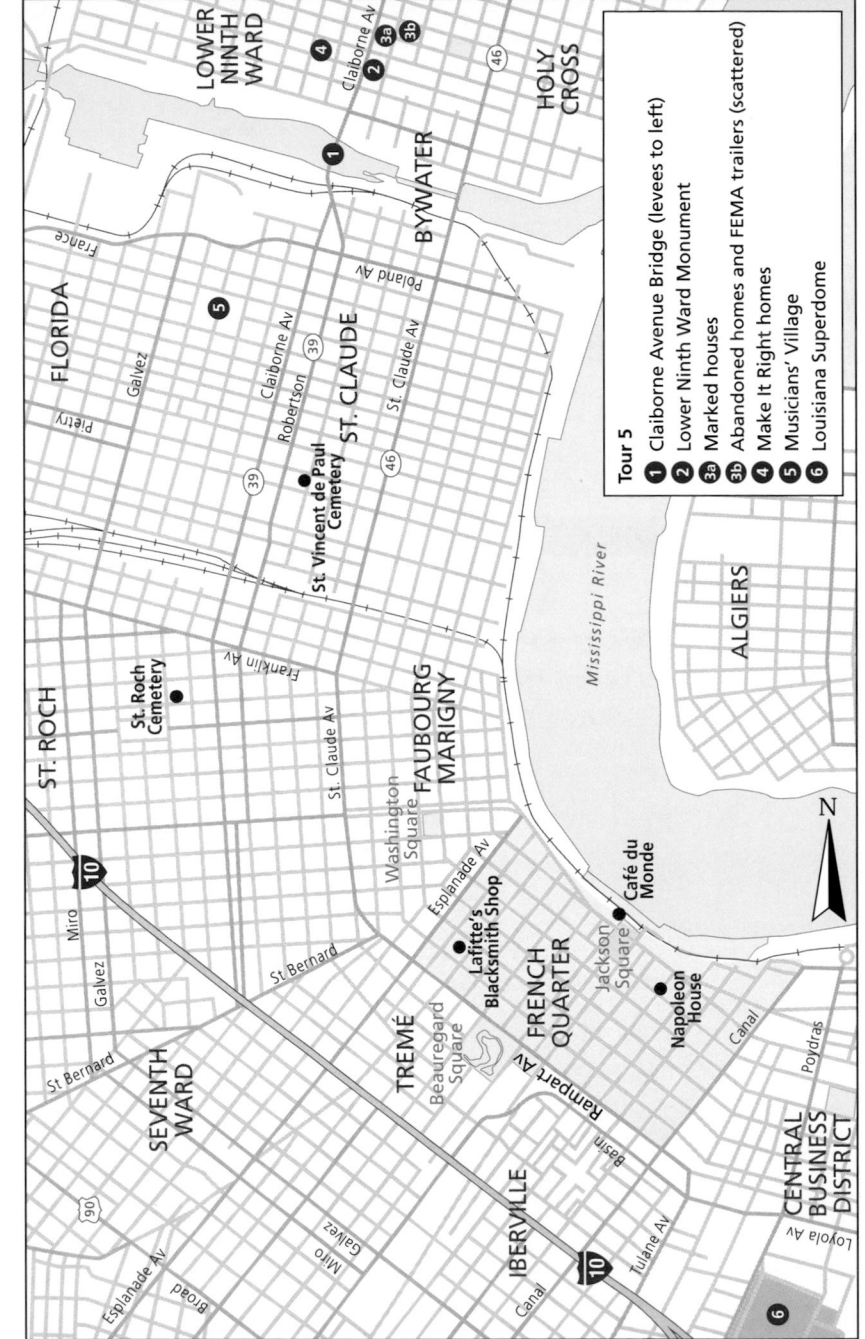

Tour 5

1. Claiborne Avenue Bridge (levees to left)
2. Lower Ninth Ward Monument
3a. Marked houses
3b. Abandoned homes and FEMA trailers (scattered)
4. Make It Right homes
5. Musicians' Village
6. Louisiana Superdome

LOWER NINTH WARD

HOLY CROSS

BYWATER

FLORIDA

ST. CLAUDE

St. Vincent de Paul Cemetery

St. Roch Cemetery

ST. ROCH

FAUBOURG MARIGNY

Washington Square

SEVENTH WARD

TREMÉ

Beauregard Square

FRENCH QUARTER

Lafitte's Blacksmith Shop

Café du Monde

Jackson Square

Napoleon House

IBERVILLE

ALGIERS

Mississippi River

CENTRAL BUSINESS DISTRICT

N

Tour 5: 2005–Now
Hurricane Katrina: The Worst
of All Possible Scenarios

No city strives to be famous for the magnitude of
a disaster's destruction, but New Orleans earned
this distinction on August 29, 2005, when the
storm surge that arrived with Hurricane Katrina
forced the contents of Lake Pontchartrain through
the canals on the city's west side. Never intended
to hold back what meteorologists call a "hundred-
year storm," the levees along the Industrial Canal
and smaller canals throughout the city's Ninth
Ward were overwhelmed by water pressure and
volume, bursting in more than seven places as
floodwaters overran the concrete levees and filled

Hurricane Katrina became a
Category 5 storm as it reached
New Orleans.

A Texas Army National Guard Blackhawk deposits a bag of sand and gravel to help repair the 17th Street Canal levee.

neighborhoods built below sea level. More than 1,600 Louisianans died in the aftermath of Katrina, and nearly 200,000 others left New Orleans for higher, drier ground in other parts of the country.

The hurricane, flood, and subsequent recovery activities—still in progress all along the shores of the Gulf of Mexico—have been called the most expensive disaster in U.S. history.

Beyond the monetary valuation, however, lies the emotional cost to people who lost their homes, their family members and, in many cases, every-thing they owned as water poured into the bowl-shaped neighborhoods and rose to 22 feet, driving residents to the attics of their homes—closed rooms from which many could not escape.

The Katrina Timeline

On the night of August 27, 2005, with Katrina gaining destructive force every hour and the storm's
trajectory clearly headed for New Orleans, National
Hurricane Center director Max Mayfield picked up
the phone and called the governors of Mississippi
and Louisiana and New Orleans mayor Ray Nagin
to warn them of the potential catastrophe headed
in their direction. "I told [Mayor Nagin], 'This is
going to be a defining moment for a lot of people,'"
Mayfield told CNN. Louisiana governor Kathleen
Blanco had already declared a state of emergency
the day before, but the call prompted Nagin to
order a mandatory evacuation of New Orleans, the
first in the city's history. Tens of thousands of people poured into their cars and left the city, clogging
the major highways and sitting in traffic for hours
. . . but in the poorest neighborhoods, people
who did not own cars and could not purchase
a bus or train ticket had little choice but to stay
in the city, moving to one of the ten shelters the
mayor opened for their safety. An estimated 9,000
people packed the Superdome football stadium,
while thousands more crowded into nine other
designated shelters on the city's higher ground in
anticipation of the storm. Others remained in their
homes, hoping that their past experience with hurricanes would prove useful this time.

At 6:10 a.m. on August 29, Katrina made landfall
near Grand Isle, Louisiana, and continued to head
up the coast, reaching New Orleans later in the
day. High winds damaged trees and tore roofs off
of some buildings, but this level of destruction was
nothing new to the city. What followed changed

A Guided Tour through History

everything: Late in the evening, the storm surge pushed massive amounts of water from Lake Pontchartrain into its feeder canals, overflowing the levees meant to keep exactly this kind of thing from happening. Levees along the 17th Street Canal and London Avenue Canal failed, causing uncontrollable flooding. The Mississippi River-Gulf Outlet, a man-made shipping channel, also directed storm surge waters into the city. Crews from the Army Corps of Engineers began work to plug levee breaches, but days would pass before they could stem the flow effectively. Storm winds tore part of the roof off the Superdome, while thousands of people waiting out the storm in their homes climbed to their attics, hoping to escape the rising waters.

The levees along the Mississippi River held fast, so the French Quarter and Garden District did not flood, although both suffered some damage—comparatively minor—from the driving rain and 150-mile-per-hour winds. In New Orleans' Ninth Ward, however, police and fire rescue units and Coast Guard in boats began making their way between rooftops visible just above the floodwaters, working to reach people who had managed to survive by cutting a hole in the attic roof and struggling out.

As people began to realize that the water was rising to unprecedented levels, darkness fell over the city—with no electrical power to turn on the lights, the night grew utterly black; with no cellular phone service, people could not call for help as they fought to survive. People climbed trees to stay above the water line, while in downtown New Orleans, 3,000 people were trapped in the New Orleans Convention Center with no food or water,

and no plan for their evacuation. That number
would grow to 20,000 before the crisis ended.

At first light on August 30, volunteer organiza-
tions begin to arrive with boats to help the police
evacuate trapped residents in the Ninth Ward,
the Lower Ninth Ward, and in the upscale neighborhood of Lakeview. Federal Emergency Management Agency (FEMA) head Michael Brown
appeared on every major network, reassuring the
country that help was on the way, but when it
became clear within hours that only minimal help
had arrived in New Orleans, criticism of FEMA
began across the country. It would be days before
the federal government would bring adequate supplies of clean water and food to refugees. Televised
pleas from Governor Blanco and Mayor Nagin went
unanswered; the federal government did not send

A residential street is devas-
tated in the Lower Ninth Ward.

in U.S. military personnel to speed the evacuation.

Throughout the day on August 30, water from Lake Pontchartrain continued to pour into the city. Rising water levels forced Tulane University Hospital and Charity Hospital to evacuate their patients as flooding shut down generators that powered ventilators and other life-support systems, but even these emergency procedures were delayed as evacuation vehicles and teams did not arrive. Reports of looting began to filter into the news media—some stories about people taking the food and supplies they needed from major grocery stores, and others about people stealing televisions and other costly electronics. Rescued survivors and others fleeing the flooding arrived at the Superdome, swelling the refugee numbers to well over 20,000—with only a day's supply of food remaining for all of them.

By the third day of flooding on August 31, water levels reached the same level as Lake Pontchartrain, while the pumps that kept water out of the Ninth Ward for decades shut down, unable to handle the volume. Work crews failed to plug the levees, and reports of more breaches came in from people investigating other canals. Buses promised by FEMA to transport people out of the Superdome never arrived, tangled in a snarl of bureaucracy; food and water did not materialize either, but more displaced people arrived at the stadium throughout the day. The American Red Cross worked feverishly to bring what food and water it could to evacuees.

On September 3, the seventh day of the disaster, help finally arrived in the form of the National Guard's mass evacuation of the Convention

The Superdome filled with refugees before and after Katrina hit the city.

Center, where the 20,000-plus refugees had remained without clean water or food for several days. Thirty thousand people at the Superdome were loaded onto buses and taken to Texas, where they would find longer-term food supplies and shelter while they waited for the possibility of returning to New Orleans, or began the process of finding a new home. Seventeen lost-children facilities were set up in cities throughout the southern United States as parents searched for sons and daughters who went missing in the flooding and evacuation.

As if to add further insult to the deeply injured residents of the Lower Ninth Ward, news broke on September 4 of an estimated 200 people who had walked across the Crescent City Connection bridge to Jefferson Parish, in hopes of finding food, water, and dry ground. They were met with a roadblock assembled by the Gretna Police, who turned back the mostly African-American refugees—many of whom were mothers with children—and forbid them to come into the parish.

Statements released by city of Gretna officials maintained that their city could not accommodate the needs of so many evacuees; a lawsuit filed since the incident alleges that racism was the true cause of the lockout.

A week later, on September 12, FEMA director Michael Brown resigned amid the national outcry over the organization's mishandling of the disaster recovery effort. On September 15, President Bush made his third visit to New Orleans and spoke from Jackson Square, pledging to do "whatever it takes" to rebuild the afflicted city. Engineers finally found ways to drain the water from the city, while the federal and state governments began a protracted discussion about which governing body should foot the bill for the extensive cleanup and rebuilding effort. With the water under control, the Army Corps of Engineers began to rebuild the levee system, with the goal of creating a stronger, more robust system that would prevent this kind of disaster from happening again.

The federal government finally approved a $51.8 billion aid package on September 8, 2005, to repair the utilities and infrastructure in New Orleans, and to help people rebuild their homes and businesses. The actual distribution of these funds continues today. While people no longer live in trailers supplied by FEMA—which were recalled because of the outgassing of formaldehyde, a toxic chemical used in their construction (and discovered in June 2006)—many homes have yet to be repaired, and more than 180,000 people chose not to return to their homes in New Orleans.

It took a year to clean up the Superdome and reopen it for the 2006–2007 NFL season. The

FEMA trailers remained in the Lower Ninth Ward four years after the disaster.

city never missed a Mardi Gras, however, and on February 28, 2006, a leaner but nonetheless festive celebration took place on schedule, with a fraction of the usual krewe members on site for the preparations. The city declared its neighborhoods open for residents' return in May 2006, and although most of the homes in the Ninth and Lower Ninth Wards were either too damaged to occupy or altogether destroyed, electrical power and clean water had returned, making the sites livable for those who could afford to rebuild. Today, we can see the open lots and the boarded-up homes that characterize the new Ninth and Lower Ninth Wards, at the bottom of the bowl in New Orleans both literally and figuratively.

In the end, the toll on New Orleans can be measured by its population. In August 2005, just about 500,000 people lived in the Crescent City. Today, the population hovers at about 311,000.

You will need a car for this tour, to take you into parts of the city that have little or no public transportation. Alternately, we highly recommend the commercial bus or van tours offered by several vendors; stop at one of the New Orleans tour information centers in the Pontalba Building on Jackson Square, on Canal Street, or on Decatur Street to get schedules and prices for the many tours available. Your tour guide most likely will share firsthand accounts of his or her experiences during Hurricane Katrina, offering the kind of perspective you may not find in books or on the twenty-four-hour news channels.

To reach the Lower Ninth Ward by car from the French Quarter, take Interstate 10 to Louisiana Route 39 (North Claiborne Avenue), and continue east on Claiborne across the Industrial Canal.

1. The levees. Cross the Claiborne Avenue bridge across the Industrial Canal from the Ninth Ward to the Lower Ninth Ward, and look to your left. The

Levees along the Industrial Canal have been repaired by the Army Corps of Engineers.

concrete barriers along the canal are the levees, which breached in three places during the storm surge following Katrina. The walls you see are 18 feet high and 2 feet thick, and gave way under the force of the water—which rose higher than the levees themselves, to a level of 22 feet. Look across the street to the empty field; on August 28, 2005, this was a neighborhood filled with single-family homes. LOWER NINTH WARD

2. The Lower Ninth Ward Monument. This monument serves as a reminder of the lives lost throughout the Katrina disaster, but also as a symbol of the efforts to rebuild this beleaguered neighborhood. Set on a median in the middle of a busy street, the monument is not meant for long visits and contemplation, but rather to remind those who pass through that this is a living neighborhood with people who hope to see it flourish once again. Intersection of Claiborne and Tennessee Streets. LOWER NINTH WARD

The Lower Ninth Ward Monument symbolizes the destruction.

3a. Marked houses. As you cross into the Lower Ninth Ward, you will see spray-painted markings on many of the houses: an X, with a date in the top quadrant. This is the date on which the house was searched for bodies, often as much as two weeks after the flooding began. The notations in the right and left quadrants tell which National Guard unit made the search—these servicemen and servicewomen came from all over the country to assist in this effort. The number in the bottom quadrant indicates how many bodies were found inside. LOWER NINTH WARD

3b. Abandoned homes and FEMA trailers. Drive up and down the streets of the Lower Ninth Ward, and see many of the symbols that remain as reminders of the disaster. FEMA trailers still stand outside of homes, waiting to be picked up by federal crews. The roof of a house lies on the ground next to a home that's still standing. Many houses remain boarded up, their window glass long gone and their structure no longer sound enough to permit the owner's return. In some places, concrete stoops and a few fence posts are all that remain of

Some families will never come home to their damaged houses.

the homes that stood there. Some families had the skills and means to repair their own homes or hire contractors and move back into the neighborhood; of these, a few built their own shrines to the ward's losses in their front yards. LOWER NINTH WARD

4. Make It Right homes. Make It Right, a project led by actor Brad Pitt and funded by private donations, has built new homes constructed on raised platforms. The homes follow the LEED requirements for green certification, and feature solar panels and materials selected for their environmentally conscious elements. Once you've seen this effort, you may want to participate; find out more about Make It Right at www.makeitrightnola .org. Tennessee and Deslonde Streets. LOWER NINTH WARD

A Guided Tour through History

The Make It Right Foundation, led by Brad Pitt, is building safer homes for Lower Ninth Ward residents.

5. Musicians' Village. In the spirit of providing for people whose interests are closest to their own hearts, musicians Harry Connick Jr. and Branford Marsalis—both New Orleans natives—linked with Habitat for Humanity to build about eighty new homes for musicians and others who lost their houses in the Katrina flooding. To live here, residents must have an income of at least $18,620 per year and a good credit history, but musical ability is not required. Connick and Marsalis contribute their time to the fund-raising efforts for these homes—if you'd like to sponsor one or volunteer to help with the construction, visit the Web site to find out how. As of this writing, 72 homes are completed and inhabited, and another 90 are in progress. At the center of the village, the Ellis Marsalis Music Center will provide practice rooms and a performance hall for musicians of the area and beyond; it's named for Branford and Wynton

Reconstruction work continues in the Ninth Ward.

Marsalis' father, who still plays gigs regularly at Snug Harbor on Frenchmen Street in Faubourg Marigny. Alvar, France, and Bartholomew Streets, www.nolamusiciansvillage.com. UPPER NINTH WARD

6. Louisiana Superdome. This football stadium was the planned safe haven to which New Orleans officials ordered evacuees before Katrina hit the city, fully expecting them to endure a stay of no more than three days through the hurricane and its aftermath. When floodwaters surrounded the stadium, Katrina's category-five winds damaged the dome's roof, the storm's force took out the city's electrical power, and the stadium's generators succumbed to the rising waters, turning the Superdome into a nightmarish prison in which as many as 30,000 people waited for days without food, adequate water, or bathroom facilities until federal evacuation procedures finally began. It took nearly a year to clean and repair the stadium, but it reopened on September 25, 2006. The New Orleans Saints and the Tulane Green Wave continue to play here. 1500 Poydras Street, near Rampart Street, (504) 587-3810, www.superdome.com. CITY CENTER

New Orleans: A Tourist's Guide to Staying, Eating, and Exploring

It requires almost no effort at all to have fun in New Orleans, a city that takes itself fairly lightly and its hospitality very seriously. Moments after you've left the shuttle bus from the airport, the Big Easy begins to work its magic: The aromas of local spices waft from every restaurant, the perpetually warm, sultry air eases the tension from your muscles, the scents of night blooming jasmine and sweet olive turn your head to inhale more deeply, the cool of the hotel lobby flows over your skin, and before you know it, you're sitting in a restaurant ordering one of a dozen varieties of jambalaya and accepting the offer of an Abita beer just moments after noon.

"This is New Orleans—anything goes!" says your server, hotel concierge, buggy driver, or bartender, and the phrase rings truer here than in any other city in the country. Here pirates once downed glasses of absinthe while plotting battle strategy; voodoo queens openly practiced their mysterious and complicated rites; the ways of the flesh were not only available, but legal; a scandalous new musical style called jazz sprang from the combined rhythms of several influences; and exiled citizens from the Caribbean and French Canada found refuge from war and perpetual strife. While cities like New York and Philadelphia typified the nation's cultural "melting pot," New Orleans stirred its disparate elements into a gumbo, each flavor holding its own as part of a distinctive whole.

Take a ride on the Mississippi on the Steamboat *Natchez*.

College students and many older vacationers come here for the Bourbon Street strip, an eleven-block-long party with no required closing time and that most enticing drinking attraction: the option of carrying an alcoholic beverage outside in a plastic cup. It may rankle that most of the legendary jazz clubs have been given over to today's popular music, but much of that music is performed live, making the French Quarter and neighboring Faubourg Marigny world centers for live music of many varieties—pop, rock, hip-hop, zydeco, blues, and yes, even some jazz. Walk the length of Bourbon Street any night of the week, and indulge in one of the best people-watching experiences you'll find anywhere: a typical night may reveal groups of giggling twenty-something women dressed for social success; grannies holding 26-ounce glasses

Some like it hot—and they find it in French Quarter restaurants.

filled with a brilliantly red, deceptively sweet concoction known as a Hurricane; people costumed as pirates, turn-of-the-twentieth-century floozies, or their opposite sex; or a bride and groom marching down the middle of the street at the head of a Dixieland band, their wedding party and guests dancing along behind them.

WHAT AM I EATING?

If Creole and Cajun cooking have not made an appearance on your home dinner table, don't be alarmed by the idea of trying some new dishes with bold flavors and unfamiliar spices. New Orleans is a dining mecca with more than its fair share of the finest chefs in America, from the most famous—notably Emeril Lagasse and Paul Prudhomme—to masters whose skill has elevated their establishments to the top of national restaurant ratings. (Choosing one of these fine, four-star restaurants may require you to pack dress clothes: Commander's Palace, Antoine's, and several others have dress codes that include jackets and ties for men and business dress—no shorts allowed— for women.)

What's the difference between Cajun and Creole cooking? This question tongue-ties even the most knowledgeable natives, because both styles use many of the same ingredients and even include variations on the same dishes. Here's the most basic difference: Creole cooking developed in the city, in the kitchens of some of New Orleans' most recognized restaurants, while Cajun cooking came from the Acadians living in Louisiana's backcountry. This localization influenced the ingredients used in each dish: Cajuns hunted, fished, trapped,

Crawfish are a staple in Cajun cooking.

and grew or gathered their food, so we find more crawfish, pork, sausage, and rice in Cajun recipes, as well as spicier sauces that can involve generous doses of cayenne and hot peppers. The more subtle and sophisticated Creole cooking involves lighter sauces; liberal use of shellfish, including shrimp, crab and oysters; and a careful balance of spices and flavors. In general, jambalaya, étouffée, blackened fish or steaks, and some gumbos are Cajun, while shrimp rémoulade, milder gumbos, and anything meunière are Creole.

That being said, many local restaurants offer menu selections that fuse Cajun and Creole, making it virtually impossible to guess which style contributed more to the dish. If you don't care for spicy food, ask your server which dishes will be most compatible with your palate. Think of your servers as your tour guides to New Orleans cuisine; they are more than happy to guide you through the process of eating a raw oyster, finding the delicious meat within a whole crawfish, or choosing the least (or most) spicy option on an extensive menu.

The Top Historic Restaurants in New Orleans

In the French Quarter and the Garden District, the concentration of famous four-star restaurants leaves visitors with a staggering selection of options for every meal, providing they have the beaucoup bucks required to dine in style. In keeping with our history theme, consider one of these wonderful choices:

Antoine's, 713 St. Louis Street, (504) 581-4422, www.antoines.com. Lunch and dinner Mon–Sat, brunch Sun. Jackets preferred for men. The oldest continually operating restaurant in the French Quarter, Antoine's first opened its doors in 1840, bringing Creole cuisine to a new level in its fifteen separate dining rooms. Classic dishes including oysters Rockefeller, eggs Sardou—involving creamed spinach and artichokes—and *pommes de terre* (potato) soufflé were creations of Antoine's kitchen, and the potage alligator *au sherry*—a sherry-laced alligator bisque—is one of the most popular appetizers. FRENCH QUARTER

Arnaud's, 813 Bienville Street, (504) 523-5433, www.arnauds.com. Dinner nightly, brunch Sun. Jackets requested for men. Founded in 1918, Arnaud's is one of several original Creole restaurants (with Antoine's, Brennan's, Broussard's, and Galatoire's) and the number of menu selections that bear Arnaud's name speak to decades of creativity in the kitchen. Gulf shrimp marinated in the restaurant's own rémoulade sauce, the white-wine-bathed oysters Bienville, on the half shell in a luscious cream sauce, and the stunningly presented roast Louisiana quail Elzey—stuffed with foie gras—make this an extraordinary dining experience. FRENCH QUARTER

Brennan's, 417 Royal Street, (504) 525-9711, www .brennansneworleans.com. Breakfast/brunch and dinner daily. Most famous for two things—its lavish breakfasts and the invention of bananas Foster— Brennan's instantly became one of the classic New Orleans Creole restaurants when it opened in 1946. Choose the four-course prix-fixe menu or order à la carte, but don't miss the delicately spiced, surprisingly hearty turtle soup—another Brennan's classic—or the lovely filet Stanley, served in a horse-radish sauce that just hints at the root's power. Your bananas Foster dessert receives its final flambé in the dining room for your viewing pleasure. FRENCH QUARTER

Try the shrimp sardou at Brennan's for creative Creole cuisine.

Staying, Eating, and Exploring

Broussard's, 819 Conti Street, (504) 581-3866, www.broussards.com. Dinner nightly. No jeans or shorts; coat and tie optional. Since 1920, this classic Creole New Orleans restaurant has presented an expert blending of Creole dishes with their French inspiration, offering both an à la carte and table d'hôte menu. Most famous is Broussard's paneed (breaded) veal Acadian, a mouthwatering combination of lightly breaded and sautéed veal round accompanied by a winning concoction of lump crabmeat, dill, butter, and cream. FRENCH QUARTER

Commander's Palace, 1403 Washington Avenue, (504) 899-8221, www.commanderspalace.com. Lunch Mon–Fri, dinner nightly, jazz brunch Sat–Sun.; closed Christmas Day and Mardi Gras. Business casual/no shorts, jackets preferred at dinner. Tucked into the Garden District across from the entrance to Lafayette Cemetery No. 1, the bright blue Victorian-style building is impossible to miss—and New Orleans residents vote for this establishment as their favorite restaurant in the Zagat survey year after year. Chef Tory McPhail insists on locally grown ingredients, making this one of the most likely places to taste the truly authentic fruits of Louisiana—including herbs grown on the restaurant's roof. GARDEN DISTRICT

Court of Two Sisters, 613 Royal Street, (504) 522-7261, www.courtoftwosisters.com. Brunch (9–3) and dinner daily. The daily jazz brunch buffet here in the heart of the French Quarter goes beyond sumptuous to majestic, turning from breakfast to lunch at midday while maintaining a stunning variety of hot and cold dishes. Choose from more than a dozen salads, boiled shrimp and crawfish (in season), eggs Benedict and shrimp

Your eggs benedict is made to order at the Court of Two Sisters' brunch.

creole or seafood omelets made to order, *grillades* (that's round steak) and grits, bread pudding with whiskey sauce and bananas Foster, and a wide variety of other dishes. There's live jazz, too, and New Orleans' famous coffee with chicory. You may love it so much you'll want to return for dinner. FRENCH QUARTER

The jazz brunch swings in the Court of Two Sisters courtyard.

Dickie Brennan's Bourbon House Seafood and Oyster Bar, 144 Bourbon Street, (504) 522-0111, www.bourbonhouse.com. Breakfast, lunch, and dinner daily. Upscale casual in main dining room (shorts permitted), casual in oyster bar and café. Start your meal with the impressive *plateaux de fruits de mer,* a selection of all things shellfish in season; then move on to one of the traditional Creole dishes on the extensive dinner menu. The barbecued shrimp arrives "heads on," Louisiana style, in a rich broth with just a hint of tangy vinegar; the crabmeat-stuffed Gulf fish differs nightly, depending on the day's fresh catch. FRENCH QUARTER

Galatoire's, 209 Bourbon Street, (504) 525-2021, www.galatoires.com. Lunch and dinner Tues–Sun; closed Monday. Jackets required for men at dinner and on Sunday. The environment surrounding this Bourbon Street restaurant has departed from its original elegance when Galatoire's opened in 1905, but this renowned family-owned dining enterprise maintains all its dignity and sophistication. The family's historic recipes continue to grace the menu, bringing the flavors of the French Pyrenees mountain range to your table with a hint of Creole: the shrimp rémoulade is classically New Orleans, while the sautéed *poisson* (fish) with crabmeat

Yvonne (a sauté with artichoke hearts, butter, and mushrooms) unites the local with the European. Reservations are accepted for the second-floor dining room; if you want to dine on the first floor, it's first-come, first-served. FRENCH QUARTER

K-Paul's Louisiana Kitchen, 416 Chartres Street, (504) 596-2530, www.kpauls.com. Dinner Mon–Sat, "deli lunch" Thurs–Sat; closed Sundays except for special events. Business casual: no cutoffs or flip-flops. This is the restaurant that launched Chef Paul Prudhomme's illustrious career and put Cajun food on the international map—and he still supplies hands-on guidance to keep the menu as fresh and innovative as it was when he and his wife opened the Kitchen in 1979. Order the bronzed swordfish in hot fanny sauce, and brace yourself for an exciting blend of pecans, jalapeños, browned butter, garlic, veal glaze, and lemon juice—not your average Cajun catch. The seafood Atchafalaya arrives in an eggplant pirogue (that's a canoe) filled with shrimp, scallops, crawfish, and sundried tomatoes, all combined with a seafood stock and butter "emulsion" that sets this dish apart. FRENCH QUARTER

NOLA, 534 St. Louis Street, (504) 522-6652, www.emerils.com. Dinner daily, lunch Fri–Sun. Casual. One of three New Orleans restaurants owned by world-famous chef Emeril Lagasse, NOLA is his most casual venue, but you wouldn't know it from the deliciously creative menu. Here you'll find that low-country favorite, shrimp and grits, but with Emeril's trademark flair with the addition of cremini mushrooms and a Creole tomato glaze. The fried chicken breast involves a bath in buttermilk, with bourbon lacing the mashed sweet potatoes;

New Orleans

the filet mignon comes with a stuffed Portobello mushroom sidecar stuffed with walnut-and-blue-cheese mixture. Emeril even turns a simple bread pudding into an adventure, with white chocolate and raspberries, topped with a red wine sauce. Make reservations at least a week in advance, and maybe earlier. FRENCH QUARTER

Tujague's, 823 Decatur Street, (504) 525-8676, www.tujaguesrestaurant.com. Dinner nightly. Business casual. The second-oldest restaurant in New Orleans—in business since 1856—Tujague's made its name on two classic Creole dishes: its shrimp rémoulade and a beef brisket in a hearty horseradish sauce. Both of these dishes are on the table d'hôte menu, along with dishes prepared from the fresh local ingredients available on any given day—so the menu changes with each day at the market. FRENCH QUARTER

Tujague's is the second oldest restaurant in the Quarter.

New Orleans Dining on a Budget

No matter how extraordinary the available dining experiences may be in the French Quarter and the Garden District, chances are good that you'd like to mix up some of these once-in-a-lifetime meals with some affordable choices.

Be sure to try a muffaletta, a sandwich invented by the **Central Grocery** at 923 Decatur Street, (504) 523-1620. A sandwich loaded with smoked deli meats and provolone cheese on a flat, round, sesame-seed-laden bun, the muffaletta's trademark is the heap of olive salad piled on top of the meat, forming a briny resting place for the top of the bun. Central Grocery serves this cold and loaded with oil, but the best muffaletta we found was the hot, toasted one at **πie (Pie) Pizza and Pasta** (814 S. Peters Street, 504-528-2743, www .piepizzaandpastas.com) in the Warehouse District. Served with a side of spring greens tossed with balsamic vinaigrette, this little muffaletta hits the spot when you duck in during one of the city's frequent flash rainstorms.

It's almost a requirement that you have a po'boy, the Louisiana equivalent of a submarine, hero, grinder, or whatever your local nomenclature for an oblong sandwich filled with meat or fish, lettuce, tomatoes, and mayonnaise. This simple sandwich got its name during the streetcar employees' strike of 1929, when Bennie and Clovis Martin, owners of the Martin Brothers Coffee Stand and Restaurant in the French Market, put together a sandwich that they distributed for free to the men who were out of work. When one of the union

The muffaletta gets elegant treatment at πie (Pie) Pizza and Pasta.

New Orleans

men would approach the restaurant, the owners would say, "Here comes another poor boy." The name stuck, and this low-cost lunch remains a favorite throughout the city and well beyond. You can get a good po'boy in a wide range of places, but be sure to try **Johnny's Po-Boys** (511 St. Louis Street, 504-524-8129, www.johnnyspoboy.com), in the French Quarter, where you'll find the greatest selection of po'boy varieties, from calamari to turkey club. When you order at the counter, you'll be asked if you want your sandwich "fully dressed," i.e., with lettuce, tomato, and mayo. The toppings are not mandatory, so feel free to ask for it whatever way you prefer.

The popular, open-air café you see at 800 Decatur Street is the famous **Café Du Monde** (800-772-2927, www.cafedumonde.com), the absolute best place to sit down with a cup of café au lait with chicory and a plate of three beignets (pronounced ben-YAYS). Close to a doughnut in their recipe, these airy squares of fried dough, accosted with mounds of powdered sugar, can really hit the spot in the mid-afternoon after you've plumbed the French Market for bargains. You can skip the coffee and choose iced tea, milk, juice, or water, but one cup of coffee with chicory may convert you to this mid-afternoon energy booster for years to come. (Addicted? Buy cans of coffee and boxed beignet mix to take home at the Café Du Monde Gift Shop in Uncle Wilbur's Store at 1039 Decatur Street.)

Beignets and café au lait—you must be at Café Du Monde.

111

Staying, Eating, and Exploring

Here are some other venues for a great meal at a reasonable price:

Gumbo Shop, 630 St. Peter Street; (504) 525-1486, (800) 554-8626; www.gumboshop.com. Make this the first place you go for gumbo, to fully understand how robust and delicious it can be. No matter what New Orleans dish you choose here—the traditional jambalaya, red beans and rice, blackened fish, or the classic po'boy—a cup of gumbo will be a highlight of your meal. The bread pudding with whiskey sauce is some of the best in town. Stop on the way out and pick up a copy of the *Gumbo Shop Cookbook,* in which all of the chef's secrets are revealed. Sweet! FRENCH QUARTER

JägerHaus, 833 Conti Street, (504) 525-9200, www.jager-haus.com. Breakfast, lunch, and dinner daily. Perhaps you didn't expect to find a German restaurant in New Orleans, but if you love a good breakfast, this is the place to try. The Schwaben Omelet places two perfectly cooked eggs atop a heap of delightfully chewy spaetzle, while Oma's Eggs bring together au gratin potatoes, ham, cheddar cheese, eggs, onions, peppers, and bacon in a fluffy casserole that will keep you satisfied all the way to dinner. FRENCH QUARTER

New Orleans

Order an omelet made with spaetzle at JägerHaus.

La Crêpe Nanou, 1410 Robert Street, (504) 899-2670, www.lacrepenanou.com. Just a block east from stop #27 on the St. Charles Avenue streetcar, this popular dinner café features some of the best cuisine we found. Try the Pâté Maison—three kinds of pâté served with plenty of French bread, tiny pickles, and olives; and the crêpe *aux crevettes,* a remarkable union of Creole flavors involving shrimp and lobster sauce. If you're lucky, the chef will offer the smoked-salmon crêpe with Boursin cheese, a delicate blend of fresh ingredients and tangy creaminess. People from all over the country told us to seek out this restaurant, and we're so glad we did. GARDEN DISTRICT

Napoleon House Bar & Café, 500 Chartres Street, (504) 524-9752, www.napoleonhouse.com. Lunch and dinner Mon–Sat; closed Sun. Bar open late. This compelling, cozy bar is in the former home of New Orleans Mayor Nicholas Girod, who managed the city from 1812 through 1815. Girod offered his home to exiled French emperor Napoleon Bonaparte in 1821, and while the emperor died before he had the opportunity to take Girod up

Pimm's Cup is the beverage of
choice at Napoleon House.

on his offer, the name stayed with the establishment. Today, the menu includes plenty of local
specialties at reasonable prices, but most people
come for Pimm's Cup, the bar's signature drink,
borrowed from the parlors of nineteenth-century
England. FRENCH QUARTER

Pat O'Brien's, 718 St. Peter Street, (504) 525-
4823, www.patobriens.com. Lunch and dinner
daily. Bar stays open "until." O'Brien's serves up
everyone's favorite bar meals, from chicken wings
to nachos, as well as a range of New Orleans'
classic dishes—but everyone comes here for one
thing: the Hurricane, a 26-ounce potion involving
several different kinds of alcohol and enough fruit
juices to make the drink taste deceptively mild.
O'Brien's created the Hurricane and sells them by
the hundred each day; it's delicious, but it packs a
wallop. Stay for the nightly piano bar—where tilted

mirrors on the walls allow you to watch the hands of the two pianists as they play—and enjoy some rollicking renditions of your favorite pop standards, old and new.

Praline Connection, 524 Frenchmen Street, (504) 943-3934, www.pralineconnection.com. Lunch and dinner daily. With all of the Cajun and Creole cooking going on throughout the city, another staple of Southern life—soul food—gets short shrift. Look no further than this friendly, casual restaurant just past the end of the French Market, a few steps outside of the Quarter. Spring for the Taste of Soul platter, one of the best deals in the city: a cup of filé gumbo, generous helpings of red beans and rice, jambalaya, greens, fried chicken, and catfish strips, followed by a heartwarming bread pudding. Then come back tomorrow for the ribs. FAUBORG MARIGNY

Stanley, 547 St. Ann Street, (504) 587-0093, www .stanleyrestaurant.com. Daily 7–7. When you've had all the Creole food you can take and you'd just like a good old diner meal, try out this little café at the corner of Jackson Square. The marble-topped tables and bentwood chairs, the padded stools at the spotless lunch counter, and the terrific service all make you feel instantly at home. Breakfast here pays homage to the surrounding Cajun and Creole influences, but with down-home taste: The Eggs Stanley feature cornmeal-crusted oysters, while the corned beef hash is loaded with chunks of pastrami and seasoned potatoes. Drop in for an ice-cream soda in the middle of a hot, sticky day. FRENCH QUARTER

SLEEPING IN A SLICE OF HISTORY

You can find plenty of national chain hotels in New Orleans, but if you prefer to immerse yourself in the city's history, selections abound in the French Quarter and the Garden District, offering guests the opportunity to stay in a historic building, an antebellum mansion, or a former single-family home decorated with lacy wrought-iron grillwork. Here are just a few of the options available:

The Columns, 3811 St. Charles Avenue; (800) 445-9308, (504) 899-9308; www.thecolumns.com. Built in 1883 by a well-to-do tobacco merchant, the Columns offers a one-of-a-kind opportunity to stay in one of the most distinguished mansions on historic St. Charles Avenue. One look at the hotel's Greek Revival columns, the mahogany staircase just inside the door, the elegant dining room, and the unusual features in the guest rooms—from claw-foot tubs to period furnishings—and you'll understand why director Louis Malle chose this setting for the filming of his 1982 classic, *Pretty Baby*. GARDEN DISTRICT

The Columns Hotel provides genteel accommodations on St. Charles Avenue.

Hotel Monteleone, 214 Royal Street; (800) 535-9595, (504) 523-3341; www.hotelmonteleone.com. Gleaming white and seventeen stories high at the south end of the Quarter, this member of Historic Hotels of America is the luxury hotel you may have hoped to discover. The crystal chandeliers, Corinthian-style columns, painted ceiling murals, luxurious furnishings and granite and marble bathrooms in every guest room hint at the Monteleone's reputation for quality, a standard followed since 1886. Recently renovated from top to bottom, the hotel now has 600 guest rooms, including fifty-five suites; two restaurants; a fitness center, spa, and rooftop pool; and free accommodations for children under seventeen. FRENCH QUARTER

Hôtel St. Marie, 827 Toulouse Street; (800) 366-2743, (504) 561-8951; www.hotelstmarie.com. One of three hotels owned and managed by the Valentino French Quarter Hotels group, this remarkably affordable accommodation with extremely comfortable rooms places you just half a block from Bourbon Street—and even with that, the rooms are

117

Staying, Eating, and Exploring

quiet. The eighteenth-century architecture lends a sense of refinement and decorum that carries up to its 103 guestrooms. FRENCH QUARTER

Le Richelieu, 1234 Chartres Street; (800) 535-9653, (504) 529-2492; www.lerichelieuhotel.com. If you're looking for history, here it is: On a plot of land granted to the Ursuline nuns by King Louis XV in 1745, the original buildings that became part of this hotel were constructed at two different intervals: in 1845 as a row of family homes, and in 1917 as a macaroni factory. Today guests can enjoy the modernization of these buildings into a lavishly appointed hotel, with eighty-six large, modern rooms and one of the most comfortable of the French Quarter's courtyards, as well as a café and lounge and an outdoor pool. FRENCH QUARTER

Maison Dupuy, 1001 Toulouse Street; (800) 535-9177, (504) 586-8000; www.maisondupuy.com. Spacious rooms and suites, a courtyard centered around a marble fountain, an excellent restaurant on premises, and a sense of luxury in its combination of the historic and modern . . . all of these elements make this hotel one of the top choices for travelers from all over the world. FRENCH QUARTER

New Orleans

The marble fountain in the courtyard is a hallmark of Maison Dupuy.

Place d'Armes Hotel, 625 St. Ann Street; (800) 366-2743, (504) 524-4531; www.placedarmes.com. Another in the Valentino collection, this complex of nine period buildings houses eighty-five guest rooms surrounding a lovely courtyard and outdoor pool. Its affordable old-world charm makes this an excellent choice if you want to stay in the middle of the French Quarter, with walking access to shops, restaurants, and attractions. FRENCH QUARTER

Royal Sonesta Hotel, 300 Bourbon Street; (800) 766-3782, (504) 586-0300; www.sonesta.com/royal neworleans. Built in 1968, this luxury hotel comes with a slice of history that's distinctly different from its older counterparts: The Royal Sonesta was part of the French Quarter's renaissance in the latter half of the twentieth century. Its balconies continue to be some of the most popular places in town for the Mardi Gras celebration. In fact, this is where the tradition of greasing the poles at the beginning

Stay in luxury at the Royal Sonesta.

of Mardi Gras first began—a precaution to keep Bourbon Street revelers from scaling the grillwork to join the party above. Today this spectacular four-star hotel offers sophisticated atmosphere and well-appointed guest rooms with all of your favorite amenities, overlooking either the streets of the Quarter or the quiet courtyard and pool. Make a point of stopping at the Irvin Mayfield Jazz Playhouse, where the Royal Sonesta brings New Orleans' own music to its patrons. FRENCH QUARTER

Soniat House, 1133 Chartres Street; (800) 544-8808, (504) 522-0570; www.soniathouse.com. With three 1830s Creole townhouses facing one another across Chartres Street, Soniat House places all of its rooms off of two fully enclosed courtyards, offering its guests a level of privacy and seclusion from tourists that many travelers crave. Every room has its own charm, from a bed in an alcove to a faux fireplace or coffered ceiling—all designed with great sensitivity to the original architecture and period. FRENCH QUARTER

Glossary

Cajun: People from the Acadiana region of Canada, who arrived in Louisiana in the mid-nineteenth century. The name "Acadian" became "Cajun" in local parlance.

Creole: Native-born Louisianans, beginning in the early nineteenth century, no matter what an individual's parentage or ancestral background might be.

filé: Dried sassafras leaves, ground for use as a seasoning. Filé is often added to gumbo.

Greek Revival: A popular architectural style of the mid-1800s, typified by pillars or columns on the front of a house or building, simple clapboard siding and strong, bold lines. The style is reminiscent of ancient Greek architecture.

gumbo: A stew or soup, usually involving a strong stock, meat or shellfish, a roux to thicken the stock, and the vegetable "trinity" of onion, celery, and green pepper.

jambalaya: A main course that appears in both Creole and Cajun cooking, involving chicken or seafood, sausage, rice, spices, and the trinity of onion, celery, and green pepper. The Creole variety contains tomatoes, which are usually not found in the Cajun dish.

roux: A mixture of lard, vegetable oil, or butter, heated and mixed with wheat flour. Roux is used as a thickener for soups and stews.

second line: A tradition of New Orleans Social Aid and Pleasure Clubs, in which the members follow the horse-drawn or motorized hearse at a jazz funeral as a gesture of respect to the deceased, and then lead the celebration after the casket is interred at the cemetery. Specific dance moves or gestures are often involved in second lining, as well as a uniform style of dress for all participants.

table d'hôte: A fixed-price menu, usually of three or four courses; literally translated from French as "the host's table."

Bibliography

Ashkenazi, Elliott. *The Civil War Diary of Clara Solomon: Growing Up in New Orleans 1861–1862*. Louisiana State University Press, 1995. http://www.geocities.com/athens/aegean/6732/files/look_solomon_union.html

CNN Reports. *Katrina: State of Emergency*. Kansas City: Andrews McMeel Publishing, 2005.

Cotter, Bill. *Images of America: The 1984 New Orleans World's Fair.* Charleston, SC: Arcadia Publishing, 2009.

Gessler, Diana Hollingsworth. *Very New Orleans: A Celebration of History, Culture, and Cajun Country Charm*. Chapel Hill: Algonquin Books of Chapel Hill, 2006.

Groom, Winston. *Patriotic Fire: Andrew Jackson and Jean Lafitte at the Battle of New Orleans*. New York: Alfred A. Knopf, 2006.

McNabb, Donnald, and Louis E. Madère Jr. "A History of New Orleans," 2003. www.madere.com/history.html.

Scherman, Tony. *Backbeat: Earl Palmer's Story*. Cambridge, Mass.: Da Capo Press, 2000.

Schindler, Henri. *Mardi Gras Treasures: Invitations of the Golden Age*. Gretna, La.: Pelican Publishing, 2000.

Souther, J. Mark. "The Disneyfication of New Orleans: The French Quarter as Façade in a Divided City." *The Journal of American History*, December 2007, 804–811.

Stuart, Bonnye E. *It Happened in New Orleans*. Guilford, Conn.: The Globe Pequot Press, 2007.

Widmer, Mary Lou. *New Orleans in the Fifties*. Gretna, La.: Pelican Publishing, 1991.

Bibliography

Index

Index